VELVET GOLDMINE
Todd Haynes

Story by
Todd Haynes and James Lyons

faber and faber

First published in 1998
by Faber and Faber Limited
3 Queen Square London WCIN 3AU

Photoset by Parker Typesetting Service, Leicester
Printed in England by Clays Ltd, St Ives plc

Photographs by Liam Daniel and Peter Mountain
© Goldwyn Films, 1998
Storyboards by Todd Haynes
"Ladytron" and "2HB", words and music by Bryan Ferry © BMG Music
Publishing Ltd/EG Music Ltd. All rights reserved. Used by permission.
Special thanks to David Enthoven from IE Music Ltd.

Special thanks to Colin Hawkins and Caroline Henshaw from
Film Four Distributors, Moira Houlihan from Goldwyn Films
and Brad Simpson from Killer Films, without whose help
this book would not have been possible.

Todd Haynes is hereby identified as
author of this work in accordance with Section 77 of the
Copyright, Designs and Patents Act 1988

A CIP record for this book
is available from the British Library

ISBN 0-571-19578-4

100242610

T

2 4 6 8 10 9 7 5 3 1

VELVET GOLDMINE

CONTENTS

FOREWORD

Mr Haynes has a lot of moxy. Todd is one audacious fellow. Mr Todd Haynes has kind of really outdone himself this time, managing to leap-frog from *Poison to Safe* to, now, *Velvet Goldmine*. Seeing the movie first should make your appreciation of this writing swell. I had to read it twice, not having seen the movie (it wasn't made yet – lucky you). It is so complete, so labyrinthine, so well-formed, so thought-out.

In Milos Forman's *Amadeus*, Salieri, Mozart's arch-nemesis, and probably greatest fan, marvels at Mozart's ability to compose, seemingly without hesitation or thought, an entire symphony; to hear – precisely and in an avalanche – each minute part, each instrument. It is as if in a single tossed-off gesture, a breathing organism plopped effortlessly and with incredible perfection out of his steamy imagination onto the page and into the orchestra pit. Salieri is forever moved, and changed.

We all know that's not how it really works but the role of the artist is perhaps to make it seem so. Orson Welles knew that and he demonstrated it several times in his glorious lifetime, also with great moxy and audacity.

Well, here it is. Welcome to *Velvet Goldmine*. As I said, I *had* to read it twice, but you'll *want* to; and the joy of watching the film afterwards is to see action breathe untold subtlety and nuance into simple – in most cases overlooked for their simplicity – dialogue and scenes that breathe and fold, one into the other, until they form a complete breathing entity, organism, symphony.

The man behind the man here is, of course, co-story writer/ editor Mr James Lyons. Together these two have created something that is so obvious in its brilliance, humor and smarts, it makes you wonder why it hasn't been here before. Well, here it is. It's funny and smart and wild and sexy as fuck. Read it fast, then read it slow. Enjoy.

Michael Stipe

June 1998, Athens, Georgia

vii

Todd Haynes

SUPERSTARDUST

Talking Glam with Todd Haynes
Oren Moverman

SOMETHING LIKE AN INTRODUCTION

'Listen – A real artist creates beautiful things and . . .
puts nothing of his own life into them. Okay?'
Curt Wild

Here are the facts as we know them today:

* Todd Haynes was born on 2 January 1961 in Los Angeles,
California.
* He moved to New York City after attending Brown University.
* He stands 5′ 10″ tall and weighs about 160lb.
* His eyes are green, his hair dark blond.
* He is an openly gay man, a visual artist, an experimental film-
maker, a student of semiology, a leader of the New Queer
Cinema, a (non-practising) Jew, a former ACT UP activist and
one of the founding members of Gran Fury, ACT UP's visual arts
arm for the fight against AIDS.
* His criminal record includes civil disobedience and loitering.
* His first film to gain notoriety was *Superstar: the Karen Carpenter
Story*, an outlaw cult featurette, in which Barbie dolls re-enact the
seventies singer's wholesome climb to pop culture immortality and
ultimate demise owing to anorexia nervosa. The Carpenter family
legally blocked the film from distribution.
* His next film, the controversial feature *Poison*, a Jean Genet-
inspired, three-strand formalist work, won the Grand Prize at the
1991 Sundance Film Festival. It also attracted the wrath of the
right-wing American Family Association for receiving a small
National Endowment of the Arts grant, deeming it 'Government-
sponsored homoerotic porn', thereby ensuring greater publicity,
visibility and higher box-office grosses than expected.
* He wrote and directed the telefilm *Dottie Gets Spanked*, about a
boy's sexual awakening and obsession with a fifties-style sitcom
star, for the PBS series TV *Families*.
* His second feature, *Safe*, about an environmentally ill bourgeois

ix

housewife who retreats to a new age colony for the chemically sensitive where she is indoctrinated with post-modern purification philosophies, baffled audiences everywhere and made it into virtually every respected film critic's top ten list for the best films of 1995 (US) and 1996 (UK).

* His new film is a glam rock epic celebrating the androgynous musical culture of London in the early seventies. It is called *Velvet Goldmine*.

* He still doesn't have an agent.

* He may or may not disagree with the statement atop this introduction.

THE INTERVIEW

The following is an interview with Todd Haynes, conducted only days after his first viewing of *Velvet Goldmine* as a complete film on the big screen.

OREN MOVERMAN: *The ambitiousness of the screenplay and the enormity of the film suggest more than just a casual interest in glam rock on your part. What is your relationship with the period and the music?*

TODD HAYNES: In 1971, the year Marc Bolan's 'Ride a White Swan' came out and began that whole glitter period in the UK, I was only ten. So I was just a little bit too young to take a real interest in glam rock. There weren't too many major glam hits that had commercial success in the States. I remember T-Rex's 'Bang a Gong' (retitled from 'Get It On'), and a trickling of Bowie that made its way to US consciousness, but not much more than that. I remember it mostly as being something forbidden, dangerous; something I associated with the tougher girls in school – the 'smoker girls' who were very in the know. They started dressing differently and making themselves up differently. It was really off-putting. America was well entrenched in the aesthetics of post-sixties naturalism at that time; kids emulated hippie culture more than anything. So, all of a sudden, this very dressed-up, shiny, cosmeticized look – along with the sexual ambivalence and ambiguity of the music – appeared and it was a little bit threatening to me.

But I guess my interest in glam rock finally arose from a new understanding of homosexuality in the world of pop culture. In the summer of 1974, while I was in junior high school and the glam rock that you see in *Velvet Goldmine* was beginning to end, I went to a friend's house and we played Bowie's 'Diamond Dogs' and Alice Cooper's 'Billion Dollar Babies', and I remember being extremely impressed by the album covers. The art was so intense! Both covers had this Gothic, horror, sexual lure to them that every teenager at some point takes pause and responds to.

I was also really into Elton John's 'Goodbye Yellow Brick Road', which was basically mainstream glam. And there was this song on the album called 'All the Young Girls Love Alice' about a girl who spends afternoons with lonely housewives and pleases them. This whole idea of lesbianism, which I found even more foreign than male homosexuality, was deeply fascinating and disturbing to me. And I remember seeing these two girls wrapped around each other, under a bunch of tarps back-stage at some event, and freaking out. The Elton John song and that image came together in my mind and I sensed there was something going on in me. That whole season, late 1974, was full of elements of glam rock that seeped into my suburban American life and intersected with my own questions about sexuality – it became a potent combination.

Yet it wasn't until college that I really started to get to know and understand Bowie, Eno and Roxy Music, the Velvet underground and the Stooges, and some of the American bands that were influenced by glam. That's when I began to see that glam was a cultural moment that incorporated a lot of different elements – including visual aesthetics – to create a very particular sound and style.

OM: *The story for* Velvet Goldmine *is credited to you and James Lyons, your long-time editor. How was the idea for a glam movie born?* TH: Jim and I were on vacation in Hawaii – we were lovers at the time – and he told me about an idea for a three-part film that combined three tales about rituals of masculinity as they are incorporated into society. The stories were about ways homosexuality is suppressed and then utilized in places like the church or the military where male bonding is used to serve a social purpose. The glitter rock scene was the third setting for the film, and I felt it was a great idea for a whole movie. The topic has never been dealt with cinematically, and it's so visual! We both earmarked the idea for each other and set it aside. Jim began to develop the film without the glam element, and we kept talking about it over several years, but our schedules never allowed us to write it together. A lot of the basic elements for *Velvet Goldmine* came out of the first discussions we had. I kept researching the subject and making trips to England, buying books and records and diving into the lesser-known aspects of the subject.

OM: *What was the research process like?*
TH: It was very long because up to 1998 there were no books about glam rock as a coherent movement, so I just read every kind of related book or publication I could find. I read all the biographies of the key artists – like Bowie, Marc Bolan, Iggy Pop, etc. I read everything about pop culture at that time. And it quickly became clear to me that glam came out of the English tradition of camp and applied counter-philosophies about art and culture, which I saw originating from Oscar Wilde. To me Wilde became the perfect manifestation of the glam era, so I read tons of Wilde – the biographies, his work, everything. I ended up writing the script with a great deal of notes and document upon document of material. There were times when just a simple, tiny phrase would make me go, 'Curt! That goes in the Curt Wild category.' It could be an Oscar Wilde poem that describes some flame-like quality that seemed appropriate for that character and I would incorporate that into a scene.

I also kept trying to broaden the specificity of the glam era to other things which I saw were related to it. I wanted to keep my mind open to other modes of writing narrative elements, including poetry – to keep forcing myself to challenge linearity and a traditional way of constructing a script. I wanted to keep pushing those narrative boundaries beyond all visual expectations. It took a certain force; it didn't really come naturally to me to challenge myself that much.

OM: *Does that challenge explain having the Wilde tradition come from beyond all boundaries – from outer space – in the beginning of the film?*
TH: I think glam rock was the first overt alignment of the notion of the alien with the notion of the homosexual – both of which

became this fantastical, galvanizing potential for musical expression, a potential freedom for kids trapped in their dreary lives. The space ship definitely brings in the outsider elements of the period, which I attribute to Wilde and dandyism, but it also refers to feelings of 'otherness' confronted at the time of adolescence. I wanted to shape that idea into a very clear metaphor.

OM: *It seems to me the doll scene in* Velvet Goldmine, *albeit brief, is the most telling of your process in writing this script. You took the icons of a certain era, much like in* Superstar: The Karen Carpenter Story, *and created your own completely fictionalized narrative based on actual events.*

TH: What I really think I was trying to achieve – and at a certain level it became a conscious strategy – was a mirroring of what glam rock itself was doing from the historical vantage point of the early seventies. The artists of that era were both looking backward into history – into Hollywood references, nostalgia, Valentino, etc. – and looking forward into Kubrickesque futurism. That's what David Bowie did at the time – he was becoming a human Xerox machine, pulling constant references and recompiling them, condensing them, distilling them down into his own narrative diagram which became Ziggy Stardust. Everything related to the period of glam came from somewhere else. Obviously, in this process of recombining and reconstructing the notion of truth authenticity gets lost. So I was literally blending the work of the glam artists with the accounts of their real life experiences and intercutting them all, putting them into some kind of new, fictional order that has nothing to do with 'reality'.

OM: *As in the doll scene, the heart of the script lies in the love story between Brian Slade and Curt Wild, who can be read as fictional manifestations of David Bowie and Iggy Pop.*

TH: To me glam was a romance between a British tradition that was extremely theatrical, self-conscious and intellectual, ironic and influenced by gay culture, and an American element that was raw, visceral, sexually potent and also influenced by gay culture. The way those two elements really fell in love with each other to create glam is personified by Curt Wild and Brian Slade. And there are plenty more American hardcore elements in the

Curt character than simply Iggy Pop, and likewise the Brian character goes beyond Bowie-ism. The love story is between London and New York, between contrasting traditions in music and style.

OM: *The narrative you constructed for that music and style is quite fractured and multi-layered. You present the 'official story' of the rise and fall of Brian Slade in the first ten minutes. Then you move with Arthur, the journalist, into a* Citizen Kane-*like, jigsaw puzzle search for the facts which, of course, is a joke since there are none. Why did you decide to structure the film this way?*

TH: From the start I wanted to set up various barriers between the viewer and the Brian Slade/pop-star subject of the film, much in the way *Citizen Kane* gives you a fractured perspective on Charles Foster Kane. It makes you feel like this person is larger than life, that he is the subject and object of other people's projections, needs, agendas and rejections over the years. I wanted the film to have an impenetrability when it came to Brian. It's not a film about what happened behind closed doors; I didn't want the film to carry a notion of objective truth or ultimate psychological meaning. The *Kane* structure really allowed me to play with these elements.

I also took a closer look at Roxy Music for examples of radical stylistic approaches to subject matter, and found a tremendous sense of mourning, longing and a general retrospective point of view in all their music. It gives it an implicit melodrama where the emotionality is not lost, despite the excessive statement or gesture. I knew I wanted something like that in the structure of the film, so the narrative could become all about the past and its lost moments. Ultimately, I think that approach enabled me to be more affirmative as a film-maker, and to valorize this period.

But the most important goal of the non-linear structure was to create one of those youth-experience films – like *2001, Clockwork Orange,* and Nicolas Roeg's *Performance* – that I remember seeing in the late sixties/early seventies. At that time you would go to a movie – whether it was with your dad because you were seven, or with your friends at fifteen – to have an experience you've never had before. You went to a movie like you would try acid; you were going to take a trip and you didn't know where it was going to lead you. That's why the slogan for *2001* was 'the ultimate trip'. It's that feeling I really miss – the discovery, the mystery that was available in cinema then, the personal way a viewer could respond to film. It was not like today's 'Will they like this movie the way they like that movie?' There was an element of excitement to cinema back then that I wanted *Velvet Goldmine* to have. I wanted you to go there and trip out. I wanted teenagers to go home and play the CD and 'analyze it, man'. I felt that quality of discovery could be achieved with some level of obscurity and that the structure would feed into that sense of mystery.

OM: *Why did you fictionalize 1984 as a contrast to the glam era?*
TH: 1984 was already a focus of future doom fantasies within glam rock itself. Bowie's 'Diamond Dogs' was the result of a botched attempt to do a musical based on the book *1984*. There was an apocalyptic self-awareness of the results of glam's decadent pushing of the envelope that was par for the course during the early seventies. That became manifest in the apocalyptic fantasies that were circulating in the London scene and I felt that they should be in the film. To some extent those projections were proven true, at least to the degree that the climate of political and cultural experimentation and social questioning that defined the late sixties and early seventies was brutally reversed in the eighties. And so it really was already a very different political scene, both in the States and the UK. It wasn't Orwellian – there was something much more garish and excessive about the period, but it was very much about power and reinstated notions of hierarchies, sexual roles, and clearly defined demographics. In many ways glam's vision of 1984 wasn't a fiction at all, it became neo-conservatism.

OM: *Where did the title for* Velvet Goldmine *come from?*
TH: *Velvet Goldmine* is the name of a David Bowie song that was written in 1971. It wasn't officially released, except as a B-side of a multiple rerelease of 'Space Oddity' in 1975. For a while it was one of the Bowiephiles' favorite lost gems. Now it's more widely heard because it was issued as a bonus track on the *Ziggy Stardust* CD. Originally I wanted the song, along with other Bowie tracks, in the film, but Bowie didn't feel he wanted to let his music be used in *Velvet Goldmine*. I think he had some other plan for the songs from the Ziggy era. It was very disappointing to me, but he

remained firm about his decision. I really respect his choice and I think it ultimately serves the film not to have Bowie's music – of course, it's easy to say that now – because, while they are fantastic songs that can never be matched, I think their absence makes it easier to make Brian Slade his own character; there are new levels of interpretation. And although 'Velvet Goldmine' is not in the film, the title was too beautiful to let go of, connoting a lot of images and qualities that defined that era in my mind. I really hope Bowie can see in the film the affection and respect I have for him. He was the most articulate spokesperson of that period; he brought the most resonant images to the glam era. Even though Marc Bolan started the whole movement, Bowie brought it to an amazing level of sophistication, both musically and visually. Similarly, Iggy Pop, who is one of many sources to inform the Curt character, is probably the most dramatic and most visual manifestation of the hardcore New York underground rock scene of the time – more of a contrast to a Brian Slade than a Lou Reed-type character would have been.

OM: *While the story focuses on Brian and Curt, and subsequently Arthur, you chose to start and end the film with Jack Fairy. He's the patron saint of the whole shebang, but he's not a true component of the narrative. How does he function in the movie?*
TH: In a strange way, Fairy is meant to be the Little Richard of glam rock. He didn't form himself like the human Xerox machine by frantically calling from everything around him and assembling himself in a self-conscious way. He represents a kind of instinctive need to camp it up, something that came to him as a young child. In the film, this instinct is represented by the enigmatic force of a pin that seems to circulate through British culture generationally. Little Richard, against all the odds of the period he grew up in – the conservatism and segregation around him – erupted spontaneously as a shrill spectacle that you could not ignore. Of course he spun right into the mainstream of society, and forced the mainstream to adapt to his new excesses. Jack Fairy remains the kind of lost originator of the whole glam thing. I think he's there to contrast the consumerist drive to be famous, which often is more effective with the very driven, self-conscious stealer of ideas than it is with the organic originator of

the same ideas. He doesn't get the same kind of attention as Brian, but he becomes a source of inspiration. He's the 'real' thing, which, of course, isn't real.

OM: *I think you would agree that the character who most personalizes the film and makes it so emotional is Arthur. He's not just the guy who walks around asking what Rosebud is.*

TH: Arthur is me. He's you. He's the fan who becomes part of the story, the silhouette who has the light turned onto him. I still have a crush on him, the character, and it's largely due to Christian's performance – there's just something so heartbreaking about it. I still can't be completely objective about Arthur. It is a very difficult part to play, and much less inviting than the more colorful roles in the film. But the weight on that character/actor to carry the film and ground you emotionally, and give you a consistent point of entry into the story – through all of these flashbacks and dizzying whirlwind of memories – was enormous. I think Christian rose to the occasion and presented us with a portrait of ourselves as the public who buys the music. The film had to have a really strong fan point of view, not just as a framework for letting Mandy and the rest tell the story. He is there for us as a reminder of our place in the cycle of pop and consumer culture, that we're really central to it. Something about that cycle – where the kiss between Brian and Curt is photographed, the photograph gets printed, it goes through the press, it gets sold at the newsstand, some little kid in Manchester buys it, he takes it home, he opens it up, and it gives him an erection – is very real. There's something palpable about intercutting the public sexuality of the rock stars with the very private, unknown sexuality of the consumer, and how one directly affects the other. I think it all has to do with the tremendous joy that rock performers get from performing their music, the sexual connection to the audience, which film-makers cannot experience. To have lived a live moment with an audience, where some kind of charge is being let out on one end and taken in on the other, is pretty amazing. It's also why rock speaks to adolescents. They are most in need and most open to all kinds of charges like that, because it's not yet codified, or genderized or labelled.

OM: *Why did you decide to let Ewan McGregor and Jonathan Rhys-Meyers sing their characters' songs?*
TH: I'm glad you asked me about that, because we have to talk about these amazing actors. I am so in awe of every one of them. In Ewan's case, I knew he'd be singing Iggy songs, and that kind of music – which is more about raw, emotive performance on stage than vocal virtuosity – needed to be performed and communicated by the actor. I've heard Ewan sing in *Emma*, so I was confident he could carry a tune, and I knew he could command a physical performance that would be very exciting. But I didn't know that he could bring the performance to such a seductive, charged level by actually singing the songs himself, getting into them, living them out on stage. He worked a little bit with a voice coach so he'd feel comfortable breaking so many rules of singing by doing the Iggy thing, but since the voice is his own, so is the character.

With Jonathan, who had to sing numerous songs in a much more controlled, theatrical style with a great deal of flourish and technical ability, I didn't plan on having him sing. I cast him for all the other reasons, but he said, 'I can sing, and I'd really love to make a demo.' And not knowing what he sounded like, I had to be very guarded about that decision. I was also worried about too many voices singing too many Brian Slade songs, that would be something that is difficult to pull off without distracting the audience. In the end people accept the many voices pretty readily; all you have to do is listen to someone like David Bowie over a span of four years and you hear the change in voice and style according to what's required by the different songs.

So Johnny made a demo over Christmas '96, at a studio in Cork, Ireland – that included him and his brothers singing three Bowie songs and one Velvet Underground song, and it was amazing. We were all blown away by it. He has a beautiful voice and an incredible command of the songs, so that ultimately he wasn't just singing the songs, he was performing them with his character's image. He sings 'Sebastian', 'Tumbling Down', 'Baby's on Fire', and 'The Ballad of Maxwell Demon' – all so beautifully.

OM: *How did you come to cast Toni Collette as Mandy? She doesn't strike me as an obvious choice for the role as it is written; her most famous part was in* Muriel's Wedding *where she played the podgy, Abba-obsessed ultra-hetro outcast.*

TH: Mandy was the hardest part to cast in the film. It's a particularly demanding role due to the range Mandy has to display as she changes from the seventies to the eighties. This type of camp female character has basically vanished from our cultural landscape, as far as I can tell. The closest equivalent today is probably a Parker Posey-type character, but she's still quite different from the Liza Minnelli of *Cabaret* or the Angela Bowie of the glam era. Mandy has a theatrical, campy party girl persona that can be turned on and off at will, and owes a great deal to the gay male sensibility of the time. I think women around the world were liberated from all kinds of highly codified notions of femininity when people like Patti Smith entered the pop cultural arena. It had such a profound effect on women but girls today have no memory of that kind of camp femininity.

I saw so many strong actresses for Mandy, both in the US and the UK, and it was really tough to find the right one. We came close a few times, but it wasn't until I met Toni that it all clicked. I had no doubt about her acting ability, but the question was how to transform Toni Collette psychically, both for the camera and in her own self-regard into this very different, very confident, overly sexual creature. She really had to go off the cliff; I'm sure it was terrifying. And what you see in the film is such a transformation, such a complete commitment to the role that she almost becomes unrecognizable as Muriel in *Muriel's Wedding*. After a certain point, nothing was too scary for Toni. What you get with the character is what you get with the actress playing her – this range of changes and the effects of various cultures and various experiences on one extraordinary woman.

OM: *Although the script informs you of Mandy being an American bisexual who reinvented herself, you get the sense of invention fully in the scene where she presents Brian with the divorce papers. She breaks down and you see the façade in a seventies context. It's a very moving moment and it's contrasted with Brian's coked-up emptiness. What did you discover in your research about the 'back-stage' women of the glam era?*

TH: I guess Mandy's basic expression of real needs is made more vivid by that scene, but the beaten-down, hard-boiled Mandy of the eighties gives you the framework for that. She was definitely one of those people who was feeling and hurting and acting out at the same time. Often the casualties were the women of the male rock world. I really feel the film builds and develops complex sympathies for Mandy that you won't necessarily feel going in. The character is loosely inspired by aspects of Angela Bowie, and it's very easy to make fun of that kind of pop creature after the fact. But in all the books I read there was no argument on how fundamentally essential Angela Bowie was to the invention of Ziggy Stardust and to glam rock in general. She inspired risk-taking and flamboyance to a degree no one else can claim credit for. It wouldn't have happened without her.

OM: *In writing the script, were you afraid that the strong visual style of the film would overwhelm the characters to the point of pushing them to the background and having the film be about its film-making?*

TH: I think the film succeeds in exploring the way stylistic tropes and conventions of expression can be taken to an extreme point of self-conscious, ironic, highly theatrical, highly worked presentation without losing emotion – but I'm still not really sure how it works. And yet it's been the thing that I've been drawn to in all my films; *Superstar* is the best, cleanest example of that. And I completely agree with you that the doll scene in *Velvet Goldmine* – which is definitely a homage to myself (somebody's got to do it) – does represent the film as a whole, and maybe in the most complete way. A lot of it has to do with the game of laughing and feeling aware of the construct – in a fun way, not in a Brechtian, didactic way. There's humor in glam rock, there's irony and wit, and it's often about its own point of address; it's often about the presentation, the inherent artificiality of our so-called natural world. And yet it ends up being very moving with its rhythm, its meter, its color. And that's something I was going to try to do with this film.

What is so hard about narrative, and our current traditions – which don't even include the musical any longer – or the codified, highly stylized pop culture of the past, is how to avoid the Hollywood gloss – which only gets glossier as budgets soar – as well as the indie gritty 'realism' we accept today. So directing this film was all about taking it to a new stylized, self-conscious, artificial extreme, without losing the good old-fashioned emotional connection to the characters. It was the hardest thing about the project, but it was the one thing I demanded from myself throughout the process.

What I really found dangerous about the many aesthetic styles and stylistic choices was the risk of alienating the characters by removing a naturalistic definition from scenes. And yet I find the 'Press Soirée' – the scene where everyone's in the gold costumes, which culminates in some strange circus/opera house – is something that carries more emotion than it would if it was rooted in a more 'real' space. And the irony is that this artifice, this scene, comes from something that really happened, that was pushed about as far into the surreal as you could possibly imagine. The scene came from the time when the MainMan management company assembled itself in London, flying over a handful of US critics to introduce the Ziggy Stardust tour. I think it was at the Dorchester Hotel in London where Bowie, Lou Reed and Iggy Pop posed all day long. Bowie changed costumes maybe four times, they served champagne and caviar and fresh strawberries, and everyone literally performed themselves: Iggy played the junky on the floor; Lou Reed played the snide American who is smitten with Bowie; and Bowie played the duchess of the entire event. It was a completely constructed theatrical performance that took place in real life, and so it didn't take that much more imagination on my part to push it to the extremes I did in the film. I kept defining the characters all the time so they wouldn't get lost in the grandeur of it all.

OM: *That grandeur, the visual language of the film, is incredibly rich and textured. You use what seems to be a huge arsenal of visual tools. Your cinematic vocabulary (zoom-ins and outs, swish pans, fades, dissolves, superimposition, rack focus, etc.), your use of color (saturated, glittering, bleached, faded, etc.), the use of different genre conventions (the biopic, promo film, documentary, melodrama, musical, period piece, mystery, etc.), and your many choices of lighting styles and camera angles, among other things, create a wonderful sense of serious fun.*

TH: A lot of those stylistic decisions came out of a focus on the way film-making styles have changed over the last thirty years. I looked at how so many of the visual motifs in those youth experience movies I mentioned before, as well as in some of the best movies of the early seventies – Robert Altman's work, Coppola's and others – have disappeared from our canvases. At that time there was a climate of experimentation with lenses and zooms: they preferred long lenses as opposed to wide lenses. It literally led to an appreciation of the grain of cinema – what isn't completely clear and completely available to an objective assessment. So I wanted to get back into that. I also had a nasty desire to break rules that were deemed tacky, to reintroduce all the potentially hokey devices that have gone out of style. I wanted all that fun stuff to become commonplace in the overall style of the film and then for it to be highly sutured with music, voice-over, and fractions of narrative.

OM: *I know you put together a big scrapbook to define the look of* Safe. *Did you do the same with* Velvet Goldmine?

TH: Yes. Three scrapbooks, actually. Big ones. It really is part of my way of working as a film-maker. Because glam was such a visual application of rock, the clothes, the hair, the make-up – both on and off stage – were going to be an essential part of how to imagine the collage of looks for this film. The scrapbooks helped inform me how the film would be shot, how it would be designed, costumed, color-coded, etc. I put together pure images of the bands and album covers, from the most throw-away back-stage snap shots to the most theatrical Roxy Music cover. I wanted to have it all in one place, to have a great source of information for everybody. We pulled out those books at every stage, from casting to costume design to make-up and hair. They were really an essential part of the process from the script stage on.

OM: *Do you realize a screenwriting teacher would have a heart attack reading this script?*

TH: I'm sure. It does break every rule in the book.

OM: *Each scene is very specific, and I remember when you came back from London the first thing you told me was that you shot the script, which is quite an accomplishment.*

TH: It's funny because I never write the script just for myself, even though it may read like it sometimes. I try to explain with the script as meticulously as possible – and it does sometimes verge on the insanely meticulous – exactly what I am seeing in my head and hearing in my ears – which includes every minute description of the score in the very first draft of the script, and all the fades and optical effects. To me, film is about all of its elements together; it's not about some piece of truth that I'm immortalizing on celluloid and which later I can finesse with clever little tools. It's all constructed! It's all working together to present to you, the reader, something that is an experience as well as a blueprint. That's where my scripts go overboard. And they often require more technical discussion than other scripts because I am paying attention to such specific details at an early stage. I don't really know how to write a screenplay without acknowledging all the elements of film-making I want to use. For example, the script would often say 'prelap', which means the dialogue from the incoming scene precedes the cut, and you hear the beginning of the dialogue in the outgoing scene. I don't really know how to state it less technically than 'prelap'. It may not make for the most reader-friendly screenplay, but it's the only way for me to be absolutely specific about what I'm seeing. In a way it's impractical; I admire the simplicity of directors who can say, 'At this stage, we just need to know the dialogue and the location.' In most films that's enough; it gives you enough sense of the rhythm, pace, the overall body of it. But my scripts are always loaded with excessive descriptions of music and subtleties that you may never even perceive when you're watching the film but that I choose to put in the writing. I have to go completely sensory in my descriptions, as if I'm describing, in semi-technical language, a film I am watching.

OM: *It probably has something to do with your need to control the medium when you direct. You also storyboard every film you make from beginning to end, which is completely unusual. Why do you insist on sketching every shot?*

TH: What can I tell you? I'm a control freak. But I have my reasons. I think most people who work in film – technicians and directors alike – agree that the clearest way to describe what you're seeing in your head is to have a sketch of it. There are so many smaller questions beyond 'Are we shooting a medium close-up next?' that describe so many different elements of shots. If you have something very specific in mind, which I usually do, you have to be able to show it. I'm sure that there are plenty of cinematographers who prefer more freedom to design things. I'm sure there are those who prefer directors who rely on them for framing and camera choices. But Maryse Alberti, who shot *Velvet Goldmine* and *Poison*, and Alex Nepomniaschy, who shot *Safe*, both liked having specific information on set. I think storyboards make the director of photography feel grounded; they show that the director does have a firm idea of what he or she wants, which goes against the biggest worry on every set: Does the director have a clue? And there are times where every director is faking it – I've had plenty of those moments myself – but the way I feel I am faking it least is to prepare as much as possible. And if I don't feel I see the scene, I feel like it hasn't been written. And if I do see the scene in my head – which ultimately I must in order to direct it – I'm going to show it on the storyboard. I have to make it visual.

Velvet Goldmine has so many scenes that are indescribable in terms of visual reality. Take the scene where the character of Devine is introduced, with that line of executives sitting at a long table. Both Maryse, the DP, and Christopher Hobbes, the designer, were very patient with me as I got closer and closer to being able to make this imaginary space concrete. It was supposed to be an empty, strange space – possibly a big studio room – but, for the most part, I wanted it to be defined by the lighting and by this absurdly large conference table that would be tilted and floating in space. That's a scene I'm particularly proud of because all of the angles, the lighting, the costumes work so well together that there is this assumption that we know exactly where we are. All the elements come together but it starts with a clear understanding among the crew of what every shot is going to look like.

OM: *In Barney Hoskyns'* Glam! *– the first comprehensive book about the glam era, to which you also wrote the preface – the author quotes Cecil Drake, Brian Slade's first manager, as saying, 'Brian despised the hypocrisy of the peace and love generation. He felt his music spoke far more to its orphans and its outcasts. His revolution, he used to say, will be a sexual one.' Is that your revolution as social activist and an artist?*

TH: What I meant by that specific line in the screenplay is very much related to the term 'the sexual revolution' of the seventies. I always saw that revolution as going beyond just what you do in bed, but having a broader notion, a new political awareness, an understanding of how what you do in bed, and who you are privately, defines who you are culturally. Taking a political stand in what you do privately is something that came out of feminism and the gay liberation movement. What interests me most about it is the revolution of identity more than a revolution of just sexuality – but, of course, they are very linked. It's all about a shifting inward of a lot of the same political motivation to break down old ideas of power, privilege and hierarchy, which had been manifested in the sixties – in a more outward political perspective; unfortunately it had failed to a large degree. The revolution got taken up in the seventies as an internal politicizing of the personal choices we make as people in the culture. These choices became as important and as politically potent as the outward, more hands-on ideas of political organization. I love that approach, and I think the effects of that revolution are still being felt today in ways the effects of the sixties mobilization aren't.

Also, I think the entire suggestion that glam rock presents to us about sexuality is one of liberation from the notion of sexuality as a fixed, biologically determined state. Like identity itself, glam suggests that sexuality is almost a creative property that we have at our disposal – a medium of self-expression that we can paint and repaint.

OM: *You've always been defined as a socially conscious gay film-maker of the AIDS era. Even* Safe, *which was about environmental illness, can be interpreted in many ways as AIDS-influenced. Was there a need on your part to return to the pre-AIDS days in* Velvet Goldmine, *to*

XXV

free yourself, in a sense, from the enemy, now that it is looked upon as less of a destroyer in the Western world?

TH: It's more of a coincidence, because I was researching the project and writing it during many of the years that we defined as the scariest around AIDS. It certainly affected so many people I knew and loved. So it wasn't a very different AIDS climate from that from which *Velvet Goldmine* emerged. But I was always aware that being affirmative in my films is something I really have problems with – many problems! I never really feel comfortable doing what I think motivates a lot of film-makers, which is to say, 'Look how cool this is. Look how cool this character is; look how cool this girl is, this relationship is, this music, this moment. Don't you wish you, the viewer, could be like them?' That instinct gives cinema a power to inform your own radicality and your own potential liberation or questioning of the world in a way that depoliticizes audiences rather than opens them up to new ways of thinking. So I've always felt much more politically comfortable making films that demonstrated the problems and didn't tell you how to solve them, but made you feel enough for the subjects who were hurt by these problems so that it became important to think about alternatives and to question the solutions. I'm always much more excited by films that give you false solutions rather than real ones – whether they intend them to be false or not. *Velvet Goldmine* is therefore a movie about what I think is truly a lost, wonderful, invigorating cultural climate. The only way I could really approach that is through concerted nostalgia which did not, and could not, include AIDS. But I don't think it came from a need to 'lighten up'.

OM: *Much of the film is about looking, about communicating cinematically by observing characters in the act of looking.*

TH: The whole question of looks is really interesting to me. I was very aware of it while shooting. The nucleus of looks happens at the 'Death of Glitter' concert where all the characters, including Arthur, are finally in one place at one time and they're all engaged in watching various elements around the performance by Curt. To me, looking at performers during the glam era was about foregrounding the act of looking and, in a way, separating it a little bit from what's being looked at. All of a sudden the way you read what you were seeing was important because it might be a little bit different from what's being presented – there might be a discrepancy concerning the implicitly theatrical part of stage performance. It might have been about the blatant sexual ambivalence that had never before been foregrounded to that degree before. It might have been about mirroring back onto you what you wore to the concert that night, an interplay of dressing like your object of desire. So looking all of a sudden became an active and politicized part of the process of being a spectator. That's what I love about the chimera between the statement, the pose, the stance and the emotional result of Roxy Music and David Bowie. Glam rock was the first emphasis on style and clothes and hair, which would invariably lead to MTV, and inevitably to Madonna, and lead us to a point of saturation with style and look. So what was truly interesting about it – the act of looking and reading – has gone away and we've lost a critical distance, an interrogative relationship with ourselves and what we're seeing. We're so used to the pose now, we just take it at face value.

OM: *Hence the title card in* Velvet Goldmine: *'Meaning is not in things but in between them'?*

TH: Yeah. To be totally semiotic about it, that's like saying there is something in between the signifier and the signified. That 'something' is culture. But when you join the signifier and the signified together as a sign, you don't see the internally conflicted components; you see it as a whole thing and you miss its potential meanings. It's like when Freddie Mercury died, and I thought back on Queen – the band, the concept, the name, the look – it took *me* (a fairly educated, gay man dealing with culture and technology and these kind of issues) a very long time to see how fucking gay Queen was to begin with. I didn't realize how unbelievably faggoty it all was, with the camp, shrill falsettos, the feather boas, the Lurex clothes, everything. Because it's become this social phenomenon that we have just accepted as part of the vernacular of pop culture, it's become a sign onto itself, it's become QUEEN! Stadium rock! It was all there, it's still there, but the shock of it, the collection of various elements within it that ultimately conflict with each other and make you think, has gone away. Often it's the gay element that drains away first. And that's a lot of what happened with glam. To me the critical engagement with constructed meanings, and imposed meanings, is still based on my desire to understand the effects of cultural production on what should be a free subject, but is never a free subject – i.e. we, the consumers. The constant proliferation of ironic references and information-laden societal preoccupations diffuse and remove our ability to be clear about the way one thing affects another. It goes against our ability to think. But I guess it sounds very old-fashioned to be worried about it at all. It's just a movie, not a philosophical investigation, right?

OM: *Maybe.*

TH: I'd like to think of it as just a movie for a while.

OM: *The movie ends with Jack Fairy singing the great Roxy tribute song to Humphrey Bogart and the theme of 'Here's looking at you, kid'. But visually we are looking at 'real' people, kids and dockers, women working in a sewing factory turning up the radio, a candle-lit bar during the miners' strike. What was your intention in taking the ending away from the stars and onto some representation of real life?*

TH: It's about emphasizing how little slices of popular culture, little songs on the radio, float through our lives, and not only bring people together in a strangely random way, but also give them little tastes of other worlds, other ways of seeing and being that we have access to through the music on the radio. That's really all it is, a slight extension, in a sense, of what the Arthur character stands for – a reminder that even though he got to sleep with Curt Wild – something most of us don't get to do – he's among the group, as are we. And that pin will keep moving through time and be picked up and passed on in many different ways. Maybe any of these people, being moved for a moment in time by the song on the radio, are potential recipients.

OM: *It ends on the words 'Fade away never', as the song fades away and the film fades out.*

TH: It's a plea, but there is something already over about that plea. Bogie was over the hill when the song was written in 1972, and glam rock was very much over in 1984 when the film ends, and even more so in 1998, even though the film brings it back to life for two hours and three minutes.

OM: *But that's still not the final note. The credits dance to the tune of 'Make Me Smile' by Cockney Rebel. There's lots of joy in the colorful credit sequence. Was the making of the film joyful for you?*

TH: I'm afraid not. But it was very joyful for a lot of people involved in the making of the film, which is a very pleasing thought for me. There's a whole complex of reasons why the shoot was hard for me and it has mostly to do with this particular script and its unique demands on any film-maker, which were further compounded by having less money than we needed to make the film. All of that made for a very difficult, extremely stressful nine weeks of shooting. I think I did a good job of finding great people for this project, and that did most of the work in terms of creating a positive atmosphere on set that was shared by most of the people involved – one of great excitement, artistic commitment and celebration of the glam era. I did beat myself up in saying, 'This should be a fun experience for you. How much more fun can a movie get?' But all the things I was trying to cram into it, and that style of excess upon excess, was something I knew would be hard to get. It was a jigsaw puzzle of a film to make. It required knowing exactly what was needed out of each piece and knowing as much as possible about the visual transitions on either side of that piece. There was not a great amount of improvisation possible. We were trying very hard to cut scenes while shooting, knowing that we were behind and we didn't have the money for the overloaded schedule. But there was hardly a scene we could cut without losing essential narrative information. The only scene we debated was the English Garden montage with the photographers, but Christine Vachon, my producer, fought for that scene and we managed to keep it in. One of the things we ended up cutting (in editing) is the final image of the script. It called for these two handsome dockers to kiss. We had to let it go because the shot was very confusing as the final note. It felt weightier than intended, although I must say it turned out beautifully. I didn't want the shot to imply glam rock made everyone gay, there's no message of that sort in the film. It was about pop culture transforming us momentarily, but it didn't work as a last shot.

OM: *The film's world première will be part of the competition at the 1998 Cannes Film Festival. Do you have a sense at this point of how* Velvet Goldmine *will be received?*

TH: I don't really have a sense of that yet, I'm too close to it, but for me there's a real sense of excitement in that whole scene. To see the film on that huge screen at the Grand Palais is really amazing. Any film shown there is made into an event. And this film is already somewhat of an event in my own mind because of the way it brings together the pleasure of music and the pleasure of film. The film feels refreshing to me for some reason, so just watching it at a good venue will be quite an experience, I'm sure. Plus, Cannes is so much about glamor, excess and theatricality, that it lends itself uncannily to a glam rock event.

OM: *There's an obligatory question in every interview of this sort relating to the film-maker's next project. When I interviewed you for* Safe *you told me you were working on this glam rock idea that was really difficult to write because you loved the subject matter so much. What if I pose the 'What's next?' question now?*

TH: I would say there's no answer.

OM: *Meaning?*

TH: There is really no answer to that question. I need to rest from *Velvet Goldmine* for a long while. It's been quite a fantastical trip, but now I need to do some living.

THE POST-CANNES QUESTION

On Friday 22 May 1998 *Velvet Goldmine* world premièred at the Cannes film festival. On Sunday 24 May Martin Scorsese, serving as head of the competition jury, presented a special award for artistic contribution to Todd Haynes who proceeded graciously to thank Mr Oscar Wilde and Roxy Music for their boundless inspiration.

OM: *What is your perception of the reaction to the film after its Cannes birth?*

TH: It's really hard to say. The directors at Cannes have no real sense of the critical reaction to a film at the festival. There's no serious discussion going on, just this frenzy, excitement and celebration that is somewhat spoiled by the need to conclude it all with the competitive aspect of it. Obviously, I was honored by the jury's acknowledgment of the film. I remember a moment at the end of post-production when I was seduced by the idea that everyone was going to like *Velvet Goldmine*. But, of course, there will be plenty of people who won't like this film. Yet I've made the exact film that I wanted to make, so any flack I get for it is well earned. All the films I've made have had major critical divides. Now that Cannes is over, and the fog has cleared, I am sure *Velvet Goldmine* will be no exception. And that's really fine with me. I hope it doesn't sound too vain, but I'm really proud of this film.

CREDITS

CURT WILD	Ewan McGregor
BRIAN SLADE	Jonathan Rhys Meyers
MANDY SLADE	Toni Collette
ARTHUR STUART	Christian Bale
JERRY DEVINE	Eddie Izzard
SHANNON	Emily Woof
CECIL	Michael Feast

CREW

Written and directed by	Todd Haynes
Produced by	Christian Vachon
Executive Producers	Scott Meek
	Michael Stipe
Executive Producer for Single Cell	Sandy Stern
Co-Producer	Olivia Stewart
Story by	Todd Haynes
	James Lyons
Director of Photography	Maryse Alberti
Editor	James Lyons
Production Designer	Christopher Hobbs
Costume Designer	Sandy Powell
Hair and Make-Up Designer	Peter King
Music Supervisor	Randall Poster
Casting	Susie Figgis
US Casting	Laura Rosenthal
Original Score	Carter Burwell
Co-Executive Producers	Chris J. Ball
	William Tyrer
Executive in charge of Production for Zenith	Chris Catterall
Assistant Production Executive for Zenith	Tracy Rowe
Executive in charge of Production for Killer	Pamela Koffler
Assistant Production Executive for Killer	Bradford Simpson
Title Design	Bureau

Channel Four Films, Newmarket Capital Group, Goldwyn Films International, Miramax Films and Zenith Present

A Zenith Productions/Killer Films production in association with Single Cell Pictures

A Film by Todd Haynes

Velvet Goldmine

Velvet Goldmine

*For Oscar Wilde, posing as a sodomite

The sound of distant waves rise up.

Other sounds emerge in succession: gunfire, explosions, rinky-tink piano, children at play, bar-room singing, opera . . . each enveloping the other like the sound of time itself passing.

We hear:

FEMALE NARRATOR
(*British*)
Histories, like ancient ruins, are the fictions of empires. While everything forgotten hangs in dark dreams of the past, ever threatening to return . . .

Sad mists of music rise as we FADE UP TO:

EXT. A GALAXY OF STARS – NIGHT – 1854

We descend, music building.

A falling star soars across the sky and explodes in lavender sparks. Purple mists clear to reveal the rooftops of a storybook Dublin.

EXT. OLD DUBLIN – NIGHT – 1854

A luminous green spaceship is just making its ascent, leaving a trail of pink smoke.

In one grand synthetic WHOOSH *the spacecraft disappears into the sky.*

In the distance, a baby starts to cry.

---

*Replaced in completed film with: 'Although what you are about to see is a work of fiction, it should be played at full volume.'

EXT. WILDE RESIDENCE – NIGHT – 1854

We descend upon a lamplit street of Georgian townhouses. The cries grow louder. A light appears in the lower part of one building. Its door opens and a Housemaid steps out. She discovers a small bundle at her feet. It's a baby.

HOUSEMAID

Lord'n heaven –

She lifts it into her arms and looks up to the sky.

The last green traces of the spacecraft's eerie glow can be seen through the clouds.

Madame Wilde! Richard! Come. Quickly!

A Male Servant appears with a lantern, followed by Mrs Wilde, a lean, middle-aged woman in a robe. They surround the Housemaid and her miraculous find.

CLOSE ON *the Baby. Mrs Wilde opens the blanket and reveals a luminous emerald pin, ornate and antique, clasped to the infant's pinafore. Music rises as we:*

DISSOLVE TO:

INT. CLASSROOM/IRISH BOY'S SCHOOL – DAY – 1862

TRACK *past the ruddy-cheeked faces of eight-year-old Schoolchildren standing and stating their future ambitions.*

SCHOOLCHILDREN

I want to be a Tailor. I want to be a Farmer. I want to be a Barrister. I want to be a Truck Driver.

Settle on the last child in the row, a solemn tow-haired boy whose seriousness is betrayed only by the cherry-redness of his lips. A hand-made name card propped at his desk reads: 'Oscar F. U. Wilde'. He stands.

EIGHT-YEAR-OLD OSCAR

I want to be a pop idol.

He wears the emerald pin on his lavender cravat. It sparkles.

FAST CUT TO:

4

EXT. ENGLISH SCHOOLYARD – DAY – 1955

The camera soars over Schoolboys fighting in a crowd. It isn't immediately apparent that a century has passed, and the child being beaten is not the young Oscar Wilde but a designated ancestor.

Seven-year-old dandy Jack Fairy is being bashed to smithereens by fellow classmates, as others circle the massacre, throwing in kicks for good measure. A Schoolteacher finally calls out and the young ruffians scurry off, leaving the boy face down in the yard.

In CLOSE UP *Jack lifts his head and looks around. He examines his skinned knuckles and notices something shiny between two flagstones. He digs between them and loosens the small object. Rubbing off the dirt, he reveals Oscar's pin.*

CUT TO:

EXT. COUNTRY ROAD – SUNSET – 1955

Crane over little Jack walking home over artificial cobblestones and a setting sun. Music swells as we hear:

FEMALE
(*voice-over*)
Childhood, adults always say, is the happiest time in life. But as long as he could remember, Jack Fairy knew better.

INT. JACK'S PARENTS' BEDROOM – DUSK – 1955

Very CLOSE ON *young Jack as he walks through the dark of his parents' room to his mother's vanity. He clasps the emerald pin to his shirt, stops in front of the mirror and looks up.*

CLOSE ON *the mirror: Jack's lip is still bleeding. He touches it. Gently, he rubs the blood over his lips like lipstick. There is music and faint sparkles in the air.*

FEMALE
(*voice-over*)
Until one mysterious day, when Jack would discover that somewhere there were others quite like him, singled out for a great gift. And one day . . .

His eyes flash back to his reflection.

. . . the whole stinking world would be theirs.

Jubilant guitars ('Needles in the Camel's Eye'/Brian Eno) as we swish to the mirror where young Jack, now fully made-up, is laughing victoriously: ZOOM-IN.

MAD CUT TO:

EXT. STREETS OF LONDON – TWILIGHT – 1974 – OVEREXPOSED
16MM

A cluster of feet, scrambling down the streets of London, teetering on mountainous footwear. The boys and girls of glitter rock are rushing excitedly over the Waterloo Bridge, across the Strand, down Wellington Street, all to see their favorite glam star perform at the Lyceum Theatre.

OPENING CREDITS

A cluster of painted faces cram for space in front of a chrome bank building doing last-minute make-up and hair; they hurry off as we PAN UP *to where someone has scrawled in lipstick:* LAST MIRROR BEFORE MAXWELL!

The five skinny specimens scurry on, passing other platform-heeled skinnies as they go. Malcolm, Ray, Pearl and Billy of the London trash-band The Flaming Creatures struggle with guitar cases as seventeen-year-old Arthur Stuart lugs wardrobe.

A lean face watches them as they pass. He turns away. It's Jack Fairy, late twenties, gaunt, striking, with old rouge hollowing his face.

Some passing glitter kids spot him as they pass. Song continues as we:

CUT TO:

EXT. LYCEUM THEATRE – TWILIGHT – 1974 – 'NEWSREEL
FOOTAGE: HANDHELD 16MM

Outside the theater we ZOOM PAST *a long line of Glitter Boys and Girls: super-foxes and she-bitches, ziggies, iggies, shags, queens, straight kids dressed up queer, all anxiously awaiting the first glimpse of glam-rock idol Brian Slade.*

6

But, looking closer, there is something dark and bruised beneath the flash. Some kids look into camera as we TRACK UP, *past their faces, to the name on the marquee.*

We hear:

BBC VOICE
(off-screen)

Tonight the streets of London are ablaze in sparkle make-up and glittering frocks as the boys and girls of the current glam-rock craze pay tribute to their patron saint, pop-star Brian Slade and his space-age rock persona, Maxwell Demon.

CUT TO:

INT. DRESSING ROOM – LYCEUM THEATRE – NIGHT – 1974

TV monitor: BBC Reporter stands outside the Lyceum Theatre.

CLOSE ON *Brian Slade (aged twenty-five), dressed as 'Maxwell Demon': his hair a bright magenta shock, his face an eerily effeminate mask. He is looking up at the TV screen through the mirror (quiet music beginning), before returning his attentions to a chessboard in front of him.*

BBC VOICE
(*off-screen*)
A palpable whir of anticipation can be felt outside London's
Lyceum Theatre as fans await the final show of Slade's smash
world tour.

A young woman with a Maxwell Demon haircut, Shannon, is shaking
a can of hairspray. Brian closes his eyes as she sprays.

CLOSE ON *Brian's hand, moving a knight.*

Security around the performer has tightened following a
recent BBC interview in which he admitted to premonitions
of being assassinated on-stage.

Shannon's spraying stops. Brian glances up to her in the mirror.

BRIAN
Turn it off.

Shannon flips off the set. There's a loud knock at the door.

Brian's hand tightens around a small rosary.

A Man's head pops around the door, the sound of the PA pours in.

9

Brian? Time.

CUT TO:

INT. LYCEUM THEATRE – STAGE – NIGHT – 1974

A HANDHELD *shot follows Brian as he is whisked to the stage in a robe. Another Assistant with a Maxwell Demon haircut hands him a lit cigarette and glass of red wine on the way. The PA bellows thunderously throughout the hall.*

ANNOUNCER
Ladies and gentlemen . . . The Lyceum Theatre in cooperation with Bijou Music is proud to present . . .

On-stage large fans are turned on, as Stagehands begin blowing white feathers into the air. The roar of the audience builds.

A crowd swarms in front of the stage. Arthur is carried away from his friends in the surge. He looks back anxiously, catching sight of someone in the aisle.

A dark figure is slipping through the chaos of Ushers and Fans toward the stage.

. . . straight back from their fantastically successful European Tour . . . *Maxwell Demon and The Venus in Furs!*

Thunderous applause as the band breaks into an intro to 'The Ballad of Maxwell Demon'. Brief shots in slow motion:

On-stage: curtains whip open as lights electrify the stage: Brian leaps into song through a storm of feathers.

Auditorium: Arthur catches sight of . . .

. . . *a shiny object being pulled out of someone's coat and aimed at the stage. It's a gun.*

Arthur's eyes bulge. It fires.

Brian is catapulted into the air, his chest exploding in blood. He slowly sails back to the stage.

TRACK INTO *Arthur, looking back to the gunman.*

A dark figure vanishes amid the sudden panic as a chorus of sighs takes over all sounds.

Very CLOSE ON *chessboard. A knight takes a queen.*

DISSOLVE TO:

Newspaper headline:

SINGER BRIAN SLADE SHOT ON-STAGE

DISSOLVE TO:

EXT. LONDON STREET – MORNING – 1974

Arthur stands at the door of his flat reading the headline. He looks up to the grey skies overhead. The sad, plaintive introduction to 'Hot One' begins.

DISSOLVE TO:

EXT. ROOFTOP (SET) – DAY – 1974

Very CLOSE ON *a young Crew-cut Boy, gazing up to the clouds with tears in his eyes. We hear his internal whisper:*

> CREW-CUT BOY
> (*voice-over*)
> Put out the torches!
> Hide the moon!
> Hide the stars!

DISSOLVE TO:

EXT. MONTAGE OF FACES – DAY – 1974

TRACK *past three young Punks, singing up to the skies with open mouths.*

New York City Drag Queens, squinting into the sun.

Two Teenage Girls in London, eyes closed, singing.

As we hear:

(*voice-over*)

For once there was an unknown land, full of strange flowers and subtle perfumes, a land of which it is joy of all joys to dream, a land where all things are perfect and poisonous . . .

DISSOLVE TO:

INT. LONDON CONCERT HALL – STAGE – NIGHT – 1972

A soft rain of glitter, sparkling through stage lights, as the song's intro comes to an end and we descend, landing on:

A glistening CLOSE-UP *of Brian, electric in skin-tight space suit and magenta shag, as he starts to sing: 'Hot One'.*

We are watching a Brian Slade promo-film (1974). CLOSE SHOTS *of Brian singing are* SUPERIMPOSED *with glimpses of his theatrical stage show, the Legend of Maxwell Demon and The Venus in Furs.*

Brian portrays Maxwell Demon, the tragic space hero, while Trevor, his sexy lead guitarist, ablaze in silk and leopard-skin, fronts the cosmic back-up band. The combination of camp theatricality, melodic melancholy and searing guitar creates a strange mix: erotic and violent but elegantly detached at the same time.

Song continues as the screen suddenly flares white.

INT. (IMAGINARY) THEATRE – 1973

We PAN *from the eye of a projector to a dark face looking up at a screen.*

Seventeen-year-old Arthur sits in the dark theater with the promo film reflected in his glasses.

CLOSE ON *a hand sliding onto Arthur's crotch. Swish up to Arthur, who sees a sleazy Old Man leaning over, smiling faintly.*

Back to the promo film.

EXT. LONDON STREETS – DAY – 1972

HANDHELD TRACK *past the painted faces of young Glitter Kids along Carnaby Street, Sloane Street, Kings Road, etc.*

EXT. LONDON HUSTLER STREET – DAY – 1972

TRACK *with Brian, dressed like a space tart, sashaying down a street full of Hustlers and Drag Queens.*

Brian walks directly into the arms of a Sailor in white and kisses him firmly on the mouth.

INT. ARTHUR'S ROOM – SUBURBAN MANCHESTER – DAY – 1972

TRACK *along a wall covered in glam posters and clippings, sketches and keepsakes. Arthur, dressed in a green trenchcoat, is just leaving.*

INT. ARTHUR'S LIVING ROOM – MANCHESTER – DAY – 1972

Arthur slips out of his room and down the stairs of his house.

His parents, Mr and Mrs Stuart, sit frozen in front of the TV. They turn in unison as Arthur slips out the door.

EXT. ARTHUR'S HOUSE – MANCHESTER – DAY – 1972

Arthur stashes his trenchcoat in the bushes and takes off down the road.

13

EXT. MANCHESTER STREETS – DAY – 1972

Arthur has a 'cool day' walking through downtown Manchester in his skin-tight lightning-bolt shirt and cherry-red sunglases.

A small group of brightly clad Glitter Kids stand around a bench, smoking and ignoring everyone around them.

The one boy in the group glances over, checking out Arthur.

CLOSE ON *Arthur.*

MONTAGE (ARCHIVAL FOOTAGE): GLITTER KIDS – 1972

The chorus resumes under a slightly hokey Narrator, as we return to the promo film with a crude but hip montage of seventies London: shots of young people sporting glitter clothes and hairstyles.

> NARRATOR
> . . . It appears today's youngsters have fashioned a whole new bent on the so-called sexual liberation of the flower power set. The long hair and love-beads have given way to glitter make-up and platform shoes and a whole new taste for glamor, nostalgia and just plain outrageousness!

CROSS FADE *with the following 'on-the-street' interviews.*

EXT. LONDON STREETS – DAY – 1972

A Middle-aged Woman and Man stand in front of a church.

> REPORTER
> Is London not shocked?

> MIDDLE-AGED WOMAN
> London's improving.

> MIDDLE-AGED MAN
> Well, I think it's a disgrace, parading around all ponced-up like a pack of bleeding woofters. Bloody hell, what'll they think up next?

EXT. LONDON STREETS – DAY – 1972

Now, a teenage glitter couple: the Young Guy talks as his Girlfriend nods in agreement.

YOUNG GUY
I like boys but I fancy girls too – they're smashing. They're as good as blokes. It's as simple as that.

EXT. CONCERT HALL – DAY – 1972 – PROMO FILM

Trevor, Brian's lead guitarist, is being interviewed in front of a small crowd of screaming fans. He wears heavy mascara and a feather boa.

TREVOR
Hey, rock music has always been a reaction against accepted standards. And homosexuality has been going on for centuries. At the moment having a 'gay' image is the 'in' thing, just like a few years ago it was trendy to wear a long grey coat with a Led Zeppelin record under your arm.

EXT. CONCERT HALL – DAY – 1972

Curt is interviewed.

CURT
Everyone's into this scene because it's supposedly the thing to do right now. But you just can't fake being gay. If they claim they're gay they're going to have to make love in gay style, and most of these kids . . . they just won't be able to make it. That line, 'Everybody's bisexual', that's a very popular thing to say right now. I think it's meaningless.

CARD

A decorative, bright-colored card reads:

'Meaning is not in things but in between them.'
Norman Brown

[The chorus continues over a final, rapid-fire collage of images depicting the ancestry of camp, fag-pop and glitter rock: Oscar Wilde, Noel Coward,

*Cut from completed film.

Liberace, Little Richard, Valentino, Dietrich, Ray Davies, Mick Jagger, Syd Barrett, Lou Reed, Iggy Pop, Alice Cooper, Marc Bolan, David Bowie, Bryan Ferry, Eno and Roxy, Suzi Quatro, Alice Cooper, New York Dolls, Brian Slade as Maxwell Demon, Curt Wild, Jack Fairy, Polly Small, The Flaming Creatures (a mesh of fact and fiction).

Return to:]

INT. LONDON CONCERT HALL – AUDITORIUM – NIGHT – 1972

TIGHT PAN *across the rapt expressions of kids in the audience, staring up at the stage.*

    MATCH DISSOLVE TO:

*[INT. (IMAGINARY) THEATER – 1984

TIGHT PAN *across a row of blank Old Men staring at the screen. End on Arthur Stuart, all grown up. This is adult Arthur, aged twenty-eight, still gangly and still wearing glasses.]*

INT. LONDON CONCERT HALL – STAGE – NIGHT – 1972

Brian completes the final chorus of the song, ending in a crescendo. But, just as the house explodes in cheers, the sound and image freeze.

A beat of silence, before:

NEWSPAPER

A newspaper flies into frame with a blast of music. The headline reads:

     'SLADE SHOOTING A HOAX'

INT. LONDON CONCERT HALL – STAGE – NIGHT – 1972

CLOSE ON *Brian confiding to camera.*

             BRIAN
         (*a thunderous whisper*)
I knew I should create a sensation, gasped the Rocket, and he went out.

---

*Cut from completed film.

FREEZE FRAME.

Image burns and is pulled from screen. White screen.

INT. SCREENING ROOM. (NEW YORK HERALD) – DAY – 1984

The image suddenly turns to newsreel tail leader as a silhouetted figure stands up into frame. The (imaginary) theater seen before has turned into:

> MALE VOICE
> Alright, Lionel. You can turn it off now.

We hear other voices in the room; one or two other figures stand.

> FEMALE VOICE
> I don't get it.

> MALE VOICE 2
> What don't you get? It was a stunt. The guy faked his own murder.

> FEMALE VOICE
> Yeah, but *why?*

> VOICE 2
> Publicity!

*[Mary, a young black journalist, steps into the light.

> MARY
> Well, I've never heard of him before –

Murray, a journalist in his early thirties, also black, is revealed as well.

> MURRAY
> Me neither.

A small, Jewish man in his seventies, steps into frame. Lou is the world-weary editor of the Herald, *a once prominent New York newspaper.*

> LOU
> Arthur?]

SWISH PAN *to Adult Arthur, a journalist for the* Herald. *He looks up.*

17

Any recollection?

ARTHUR

Of *what*?

LOU

This – Slade fellow?

ARTHUR
(*frowning*)

Vaguely.

LOU
(*victory*)

Vaguely! There you go!

Lou and the others all look at Arthur.

ARTHUR
(*grumpy with the attention*)

What? Early seventies . . . glam-rock singer?

*[MARY

What rock?

LOU

Glam. As in 'glamor'. Also known as *glitter* rock –
(*turns to Arthur*)

Yes?

Arthur shrugs vaguely as Lou continues, walking to the window, faint music hovering.

A brief, largely British trend. Known for its flamboyance.
Artists like, Brian Slade, Jack Fairy, uhhhhhhhh . . . what's-his-name?

Lou looks to Arthur, searching for a name, music tensing.

Curt Wild!

Arthur, CLOSE, *flinches softly.*

CLOSE ON: *Lou, who seems to notice. He continues.*

*Cut from completed film.

18

But short-lived. Following the whole shooting stunt fans lost interest –

> ARTHUR
> (*still sullen*)
> Lost *interest* – they burned his bloody records in the street.]

> MURRAY
> Told you we could count on Mr Old-Time Rock and Roll!

He and Mary snicker.

> ARTHUR
> (*turning to Lou*)
> Count on me for *what*?
> (*to Lou*)
> I thought I was on the Reynolds trip.

> LOU
> You are. But the President isn't due till the eighth and we need a piece for the *Weekender now*.

> ARTHUR
> (*quiet, facetious*)
> Great.

> MARY
> Hey – I had the last *three Weekenders*!

> LOU
> Look. Next week is the tenth year anniversary of the whole stunt shooting incident. Find out what happened. Who knew him. Where he is today. 'What Ever Happened To Brian Slade?' The Rise and Fall. Alright? Four thousand words.

Arthur looks away, shaking his head.

> ARTHUR
> And naturally you want me for this because I'm the resident Brit, right?

> LOU
> No.

Arthur stops.

I want you because you remember.

A dramatic BOOM.

CUT TO:

EXT. NEW YORK PANORAMA – DAY – 1984

The burnt-out remains of New York City and the subtitle:

NEW YORK CITY, 1984

1984 New York is a decadent, seventies vision of an apocalyptic future: a bombed-out, expressionistic city from which most people, wealthy or white, have already fled.

Melancholy music.

EXT. NEW YORK STREETS – DAY – 1984

Arthur walks home through a blue-gel twilight. Pulling out, we reveal a grey, industrial landscape, emptied of color and life. A small line of National Guards patrol the area.

ARTHUR
(*voice-over*)
Some meaningless prank, a decade old. Why was it suddenly up to me to figure it out when clearly there was something, something from the past spooking me back? I didn't realize at the time that it was you.

Rising in the distance, we hear the rumble of a crowd and the echoey bass of stadium rocker Tommy Stone's song 'People Rockin' People' over loudspeaker. A Man's voice follows, massive with echo.

MALE VOICE
Thank you Transelectric and CRA. MicroAtlanta and Dupree for their generous support.

DISSOLVE TO:

EXT. COURTHOUSE – NEW YORK – DAY – 1984

TRACK OVER *the heads of a crowd of mostly kids, gathered around an enormous screen. Tommy Stone, a bleach-blond corporate superstar, is*

20

being simulcast from a distant stadium filled with bleach-blond fans.

Music continues under:

> TOMMY STONE
> *(on TV)*
> Thanks to President Reynolds' Committee for Cultural
> Renewal for making this broadcast possible and thanks to
> you, the three billion viewers tuning in right now on global
> satellite . . .

CLOSE ON: *Arthur as the booming telecast fades and he descends the subway stairs.*

INT. SUBWAY STAIRS – NEW YORK – DAY – 1984

A dark figure whisks by.

There is a sudden chill of music as Arthur turns.

The man passing, a sinewy character in his late thirties, flashes a cool glance at Arthur before rushing out of sight. (We don't know it yet but this is Curt Wild.)

Very CLOSE ON *Arthur, struck, as the roar of an oncoming train rises with the music.*

> DISSOLVE TO:

INT. SUBWAY – NEW YORK – DAY – 1984

A packed subway car, gnarled with damage and black with graffiti, flickers in and out of darkness. People are tossed against each other but everyone is so deep in thought no one seems to notice.

We hear:

> CHILD'S VOICE
> 'Yesterday upon the stair
> I saw a man that wasn't there'

A small Black Child in a Tommy Stone mask, is reading to her mother from a book.

'He wasn't there again today
How I wish he'd go away.'

CLOSE ON *Arthur, listening. He turns and looks out his window.*

Arthur's reflection through flickering glimpses into passing trains: sad faces looking out.

ARTHUR
(*voice-over*)
Ten years. Ten years and the world had changed so completely that the life I led in England seemed like someone else's life. Someone else's story. Anyone's but mine.

Out of the melancholy of the score, a song from the past begins to rise. ('Avenging Annie'/Andy Pratt).

DISSOLVE TO:

EXT. PASSING STREETS OF SUBURBAN MANCHESTER – DAY – 1973

MALE TEACHER
(*off-screen*)
'There were times when it appeared to Dorian Gray that the whole of history was merely a record of his own life,'

EXT. SCHOOLYARD – MANCHESTER SUBURBS – DAY – 1973

Three Kids in glitter-rock gear are running late to class, laughing and tripping on their flashy footwear. One of them is the Glitter Boy seen earlier.

MALE TEACHER
(*off-screen*)
'not as he had lived it in act and circumstance, but as his imagination had created it for him, as it had been in his brain and in his passions.'

INT. CLASSROOM – MANCHESTER – DAY – 1973

Teenage Arthur watches the kids through his classroom window. He returns his attention to his meticulous rendering on an exercise book of Brian Slade as Maxwell Demon.

The off-screen voice of the Teacher continues with the music.

> TEACHER
> 'He felt that he had known them all, those strange, terrible figures that had passed along the stage of life, and made sin so marvelous and evil so full of subtlety.'

Suddenly Arthur looks up. Music stops. His Teacher is looking right at him. 'Coz I Luv You'/Slade begins.

> 'It seemed that in some mysterious way, their lives had been his own . . .'

Music rises in volume with:

CUT TO:

INT. RECORD STORE – MANCHESTER – DAY – 1973

We TRACK *past the display of recent releases: Spinners, Gilbert O'Sullivan, The Carpenters, etc.*

Teenage Arthur searches pensively for a certain release. Then he spots it.

CLOSE ON *the Brian Slade album,* The Ballad of Maxwell Demon. *He gingerly reaches for a copy.*

Arthur turns solemnly and begins approaching his Brother, who is standing with two Friends by the cash register, arguing over boy bands.

> FRIEND I
> . . . That's a load of crap – Blind Faith takes the piss out of Dereck and the Dominoes –

> BROTHER
> *Bollocks!*

> FRIEND 2
> Sod off, man! The Yardbirds blow both of them out of the water –

Arthur approaches his brother who stands with one long-haired friend chatting to another behind the counter.

23

FRIEND I

You and Nigel, man – it's like the fuckin' Yardbirds were the only fuckin' band that ever existed –

FRIEND 2

And we'd be fuckin' right then!

FRIEND I

Paul, you're thick as pig shit, you are –

Arthur stands opposite his brother.

ARTHUR

Nigel. Can you lend us two quid? I got money at home.

BROTHER

You must be mental.

ARTHUR

Pleeease! I swear I have it!

BROTHER

Oh piss off – what for then?

ARTHUR

Nothing.

> BROTHER

Give us it here. Let's have a look.

Arthur's brother grabs the album out of his hands.

Bloody Nora!

Music rises as Arthur's brother shows the record to his friends.

Our kid's one of them pansy rockers!

> FRIEND 1

Fuckin' hell!

> FRIEND 2
> (*pointing to record*)

He's a fucking poof, that one there.

Arthur is completely confused.

> ARTHUR

No he's not! That's naff.

> FRIEND 1

That's naff.

> BROTHER
> (*to Arthur*)

You're disgustin' – you know that?

CLOSE ON *Arthur, purple with instinctive shame. Music rises.*

CUT TO:

EXT. ARTHUR'S STREET – MANCHESTER – AFTERNOON – 1973

CLOSE UP TRACK *with Arthur as he lumbers home, deep in thought, trying to figure it all out. Slow pan down reveals the record under his arm.*

EXT. ARTHUR'S HOUSE – MANCHESTER – AFTERNOON – 1973

Continuous crane up as Arthur approaches his house and hurries in, slamming the door behind him.

CUT TO:

A series of brief, CLOSE SHOTS:

INT. ARTHUR'S BEDROOM – MANCHESTER – DAY – 1973

Arthur jams the door with a chair.

Album Cellophane is peeled and crumpled.

A shiny record is slid out of its sleeve and placed on to a turntable.

The needle drops and glides into its groove, filling the room with a glorious, anticipatory hiss.

'Hot One' begins.

Arthur opens up his new copy of the Melody Maker.

CLOSE ON *the newsprint pages. Arthur turns to a fold-out spread on Brian Slade's stage persona Maxwell Demon.*

He stares endlessly at the skin-tight androgyny in each juicy still.

He turns the page, revealing a large black-and-white blow-up of Brian Slade and Curt Wild kissing hotly on the mouth.

CLOSE ON *Arthur's face, confused and shocked.*

FAST CUT TO:

INT. SUBWAY CAR – NEW YORK – DUSK – 1984

Adult Arthur staring out of a subway car, stopped at a station.

Arthur looks out on to the station platform. The doors begin to close.

Suddenly Arthur realizes what stop it is and scrambles for the door.

Music rises ('The Fat Lady of Limbourg'/Brian Eno) with the sound of a seventies news broadcast:

> NEWSCAST
> (*voice-over*)
> Today in London officials confirmed that the February 5th shooting of singer Brian Slade at London's Lyceum Theatre *was* a publicity stunt, mounted by the singer's company, Bijou Music Limited.

NEWSPAPER ON MICROFILM

A 1974 headline reads:

> 'BRIAN SLADE SHOOTING DECLARED A HOAX'

TRACK IN *to story below, subtitled:*

> 'BETRAYED FANS STRIKE OUT'

INT. NEWSROOM LIBRARY – NIGHT – 1984

Slow TRACK IN *to Arthur reading the story, colorless in the negative light.*

> NEWSCAST
> (*voice-over*)
> Manager Jerry Devine announced today that his company meant 'no harm' in their 'escapades', that it was intended solely as 'entertainment' . . .

The sound of the newscast cross-fades with that of Jerry Devine, Brian's manager.

EXT. BIJOU OFFICES – DAY – 1974 – NEWSREEL FOOTAGE:
HANDHELD 16MM

Devine speaks to a camera crew as he walks from his car up the steps of his Chelsea office building. An OFFICES FOR RENT *sign can be seen behind him.*

> DEVINE
> Very unfortunate and sad that, in this day and age, an artist's quest for artistic freedom should cost him his career.

CUT TO:

INT. WEST BERLIN CAFÉ – DAY – 1974 – NEWSREEL FOOTAGE

Curt Wild is being interviewed by a German television crew in a modern Kaffee Haus. Beside him at the bright-red table sits Jack Fairy.

> INTERVIEWER
> (*off-screen*)
> Warum, denken Sie? Warum –

> TRANSLATER
> (*off-screen*)
> Why do you think?

A card reads: CURT WILD – JACK FAIRY – WEST BERLIN

> CURT
> (*irritably*)
> I have no idea why. It just got too big, too schizoid, the whole thing, I mean . . . He thought he [beeep]-ing *was* Maxwell Demon by the end – you know? And it's like – Maxwell Demon thought he was God.

BACK TO:

INT. NEWSROOM LIBRARY – NIGHT – 1984

Music continues as Arthur scans through another roll of microfilm.

A montage of headlines.

'BRIAN SLADE SALES PLUMMET'

'BRIAN SLADE UK TOUR CANCELLED'

'SINGER BRIAN SLADE SCHEDULED TO HOST TEEN POPSWOP
AWARDS'

'SINGER BRIAN SLADE CHARGED WITH COCAINE POSSESSION'

DISSOLVE TO:

Reference book.

*We follow Arthur's finger as he scrolls down a periodicals listing for
Brian Slade. After 1974 references are scarce. Arthur's finger stops at the
last date: September 1977.*

He looks up, pensive. Music is suspicious.

We hear:

> MALE VOICE
> (*off-screen*)
> Brian Slade? Oh yes.

Briefly:

BEDROOM – DAY – 1969 – SILENT SUPER-8

*Grainy image of two men having sex in morning light – one of them is
Brian.*

FAST CUT TO:

INT. CITY HOSPITAL, NEW YORK – DAY – 1984

CLOSE ON *the unshaven face of a fifty-three-year-old Cecil Drake,
Brian's first manager, remembering.*

> CECIL
> Quite well. Quite well.

Arthur stands opposite with a notepad.

> Once upon a time.

*With that Cecil pivots around in his wheelchair and takes off down the
narrow corridor of the decrepit city hospital.*

Arthur scurries after, calling out as he goes:

ARTHUR

So?

CECIL

Yes?

ARTHUR

What was he – what was he like?

CECIL

Who's that – Brian?

ARTHUR

Yes –

Cecil makes a sudden turn off near the elevators.

Arthur turns and follows.

CLOSE ON *Cecil facing a dirty window, suddenly quite still.*

CECIL
(*quietly*)
Like nothing I'd ever seen before.

Arthur stands behind, watching him.

And in the end . . . like nothing he appeared.

A quiet draw of music pulls Arthur on to a seat opposite.

SLOW TRACK *into Cecil, recalling a quotation:*

He was elegance, walking arm in arm with a lie.

Music blooms.

DISSOLVE TO:

INT. BRIAN'S BEDROOM – BIRMINGHAM – DAY 1956

Slow TRACK *past the face of an angelic seven-year-old boy, combing his hair in the mirror with steely concentration. Brian Slade, immaculately dressed, puts down the comb and stares at his perfect reflection.*

CECIL
(*voice-over*)
His real name, in fact, was Thomas, and his father owned a
small tiling business in suburban Birmingham. But Brian
never cared much for the suburbs and, as a young boy, had
the rare fortune of spending a summer in London with his
aunt –

CUT TO:

INT. MUSIC HALL – LONDON – NIGHT – 1956

TRACK *along the floorboards of a last-legs music-hall, where a smoky
vaudeville act is glimpsed through fringed curtains and footlights.*

*Brian is creeping along the rim of the orchestra pit, observing show and
backstage antics alike.*

CECIL
(*voice-over*)
– a figure of some ill repute in the Slade family, after she
married a cockney in the 'entertainment field' and followed
him off to Deptford.

*Backstage, Brian spots his fat, mustached Uncle, the director, ordering
people around in a sweaty huff.*

*Brian settles into a sliver of light and watches the rest of the performance
with intensity.*

*The wiggly, over-painted Singer (a pantomime dame stuffed into a
bustier), is belting out a saucy number. Behind her, three Girls in stripes
make up the swimsuit chorus.*

CUT TO:

INT. BACKSTAGE – MUSIC HALL – NIGHT – 1956

*A comedian with zany sound-effects is heard in the distance as Brian
tiptoes up a dark stairway.*

*At the top of the stairs he spots a dressing-room door, partly open. From
inside, he hears the sound of a woman in distress.*

Cautiously, he approaches. He peers in through the crack.

All we see is a woman's red-nailed hand pushing against a large man.

Brian inches the door open for a better view.

INT. DRESSING ROOM – MUSIC HALL – NIGHT – 1956

His fat Uncle, in CLOSE-UP, *spots him and winks. Quick zoom out, revealing him seated on a dressing table, pants open, with the head of the Transvestite Singer between his legs, in the throes of fellatio.*

Brian stares in shock.

> CECIL
> (*voice-over*)
> Brian's tender introduction to the theatrical underworld would leave a dramatic impression.

His Uncle blows the boy a little kiss.

Brian's eyes bulge. We hear a high-pitched, Little Richard squeal.

WILD SWISH PAN TO:

INT. STONE LIVING ROOM – EVENING – 1956

With a musical bang, Brian (aged seven) slides into frame, dressed in a black pompadour wig and make-up – as Little Richard. He performs 'Tutti Fruiti' in his own piercing falsetto, singing the song with its 'original' lyrics, and playing up each sexual innuendo with broad, Little Richard gestures.

> BRIAN
> (*sings*)
> A wop bop a lu bop a wop bam boom (*etc.*)

At the end of the song Little Brian finishes with a saucy bang.

FAST CUT TO:

INT. STONE LIVING ROOM – EVENING – 1956

Brian's Parents, Gran and Brother sit watching, dumbstruck, as 'Do You Wanna Touch Me (Oh Yeah)'/Gary Glitter begins.

CUT TO:

EXT. BIRMINGHAM STREET – DAY – 1965

Brian Slade (aged sixteen), the perfect mod, is in the midst of deep-mouth kissing his perfect Mod Girlfriend. He wears a short jacket, tight trousers, and has a puffed bouffant – dyed blond and lacquered.

As they finish, she asks:

> MOD GIRLFRIEND
> So what are you, a mod or a rocker?

> BRIAN
> Six of one, half a dozen of the other, really.

Brian winks, pecks her on the cheek and we pull out. The Mod Girlfriend gets on her bicycle and rides off. Brian waves goodbye and turns, checking his face in a pocket mirror as he joins two other Mod Boys, leaning against a wall, posing with fags.

A pack of uniformed Schoolboys are passing.

> CECIL
> (*voice-over*)
> Taking their cue from Little Richard, the swank London mods – short for modernists – were the first to wear mascara and lacquer their hair, the first true dandies of pop –

One pretty Tow-haired Boy, busily winding a bright gold watch, lags behind the rest.

Brian notices him pass.

> – and known to just about any indiscretion where a good suit was involved.

The Tow-haired Boy stops and looks over his shoulder at Brian.

CUT TO:

INT. BRIAN'S BEDROOM – BIRMINGHAM – DAY – 1965

CLOSE PAN UP *Brian, slipping the gold watch into his pocket and removing his tie. His eyes are fixed on something below him.*

Full shot: Brian stands opposite the Boy, spread out on his bed, face down and bare-bottomed.

> CECIL
> (*voice-over*)
> Style always wins out in the end.

Brian's tie drops to the floor.

Freda Payne 'Band of Gold'.

CUT TO:

INT. SOMBRERO CLUB – LONDON – NIGHT – 1971

A Drag Singer lip-syncs with the song, on a small club stage draped in silver spangles.

> CECIL
> (*voice-over*)
> For Brian, the mods were a glamoros call to arms – or at least, to London, where, three years later, at the Sombrero Club in Kensington,

Cecil sits with two middle-aged gay friends at a table.

> I would hear him sing for the very first time.

The Singer finishes and the club cheers. Packed to the gills; the streaming club swarms with the finest of London trash and glamour.

> Everything, it seemed, started at the Sombrero. No club in London had more notorious sway. And there, at the center of it, was Brian's American wife, Mandy, who's dramatic transformation to London party girl was a constant source of amusement to us all.

> MANDY
> You all know me – subtlety's my middle name. It's as subtle as the piece of skin between my vagina and my anus – ooh la! la!
> (*laughter*)
> Now what's that *called*, I can never quite remember . . . No man's land!? Oh gosh – my geesh! *Now*: ladies and

34

gentlemen, boys and girls – and whomever else may be in the house this evening . . .

The club starts to clap and cheer.

It is my supreme pleasure to introduce all you lovelies here tonight to the Sombrero Club's prettiest star – and my most shimmering hubby! – *Brian Slade!*

Brian walks out from the shimmer of spangle drapes, swathed in satin and pearl like a pantomime damsel. His hair at this point is long and straight and parted on the side like Lauren Bacall.

He and Mandy kiss and raise their joined hands: the perfectly androgynous, bisexual couple of the seventies. Music begins as curtains lift behind them, revealing Brian's small back-up band playing against the shimmer of spangle drapes. Mandy walks off and Brian steps to the mike, performing '2HB'/Roxy Music.

Cecil stares in quiet, amorous shock while his companions make the customary cracks.

FRIEND 1
Ooo, varda Mistress Bona!
(Subtitle reads: 'Say, have a look at "Miss Beautiful"!')

FRIEND 2
Varda the omie palome!
(Subtitle: 'Have a look at the homosexual!')

FRIEND 1
A tart, my dears, a tart in gildy clobber!
(Subtitle: 'A slut, mates, a slut in fancy clothes!')

Cecil is captivated.

CECIL
Who is he?

Friend 1 is suddenly at one ear.

FRIEND 1
A scrubber, my dear, I assure you.

With Friend 2, at the other.

35

FRIEND 2

Though not too scruffy as I recall.

FRIEND I

You're wicked.

Cecil tosses a smirk at both of them and stands. He straightens his blazer and heads off towards the stage for a better view.

Cecil's friends watch him go, incredulous.

FRIEND I

She won't be home tonight.
        (Subtitle: 'He won't be home tonight.')

CECIL
(*voice-over*)

So I introduced myself. Told him I was developing my own management company, and on the look-out for new talent. He introduced me to his wife, asked me what sign I was, and before the week was out – we were signing contracts.

Brian catches sight of Cecil and gives him a little smile.

You see, Brian believed in the future.

Music rises over:

CUT TO:

MONTAGE (ARCHIVAL FOOTAGE): LONDON HIPPIES

We see footage of late sixties hippie culture.

> CECIL
> (*voice-over*)
> He despised the hypocrisy of the peace and love generation
> and felt his music spoke far more to its orphans and its
> outcasts. *His* revolution, he used to say, will be a sexual one.

DISSOLVE TO:

EXT. OUTDOOR CONCERT – SOUTH-WEST ENGLAND – DAY – 1971

We TRACK *over a mass of grungy hippies, gathered for an all-day
concert, staring at the stage with perplexed expressions (slight* SLOW
MOTION).

> CECIL
> (*voice-over*)
> But in 1970, rock audiences bred on Credence Clearwater and
> the Beatles were not entirely sure what to make of this
> particular brand of revolt.

*On-stage, under a large yellow canopy, Brian performs a song
('Sebastian'/Cockney Rebel) on piano in a scarf and with a white face,
still with long hair. Wearing a long velvet dress and suede boots, he
sings with far greater affectation than before. For a moment it appears
as if he's become Jack Fairy.*

*Cecil and Mandy watch from the audience. In front of them, a Hippie is
joined by his Hippie Friend.*

> HIPPIE FRIEND
> Who's this geezer, then?

> HIPPIE
> Some shirt-lifter from Birmingh'm.

37

CUT TO:

INT. HOSPITAL – NEW YORK – DAY – 1984

CECIL

Somehow he got it into his head that he had to perform in a frock – Don't ask me why. I mean, I thought it was a bit naughty, a bit of a giggle, but . . .

RETURN TO:

EXT. OUTDOOR CONCERT – DAY – 1971

Hisses from the audience, followed by a few shouts.

AUDIENCE

Get the fuck off! Cut the shite! Bugger off, you wooftah!

Brian struggles to finish, glancing over to Cecil in the audience.

*[CECIL
                   (*voice-over*)
Let's just say he'd not quite set the world on fire as yet.]

CUT TO:

BACKSTAGE – OUTDOOR CONCERT – LATE DAY – 1971

Mandy is a gush of enthusiasm as she and Cecil trail Brian, who quickly collects his belongings. Hard rock on the PA billows from the stage.

MANDY

Darling, darling you were fabulous! Every bit! I was *beaming* – truly – like someone's mum. And they adored you! The whole lot – transported!

BRIAN
(*to Cecil*)
Transported! – We went down like a fuckin' knackered lift!

*Cut from completed film.

38

CECIL

Brian, I tell you, I think it's simply a matter of presentation, and that with proper back-up –

BRIAN

Back-up! What happened to Judy Garland! What happened to all your bloody torch song rubbish!

CECIL

In a cabaret, *yes*! But in the context of a rock show, I see now it's a bit more dodgy. But the act is *there*. *All* it needs –

Blaring from the stage, the Announcer's voice on the PA:

ANNOUNCER
(*off-screen*)

Next up, all the way from New York City –

BRIAN

Let's blow –

ANNOUNCER
(*off-screen*)

– lead singer and founder of the greatest garage band known to mankind . . . on his own for the very first time – *Curt Wild*!

CUT TO:

EXT. OUTDOOR CONCERT – NIGHT – 1971

Brian, Mandy and Cecil are walking out as a deep, brooding guitar begins.

Brian can't help but look.

On-stage, a dark figure appears. Track in, music rising.

Briefly:

INT. HOSPITAL – NEW YORK – DAY – 1984

Arthur looks up at Cecil, CLOSE.

CECIL
(*to camera*)

Curt Wild.

FAST RETURN:

EXT. OUTDOOR CONCERT – STAGE – NIGHT – 1971

Lights and a bolt of guitars ignite the stage ('TV Eye'/The Stooges.) Curt Wild, aged twenty-five, wearing a twisted rag around his waist, lifts a can of oil into the air and starts covering himself with its threads.

Brian has stopped, stricken by what he sees. Slow TRACK IN.

Curt throws the oil away and begins rubbing his glistening body and groin along to the words.

CECIL
(*voice-over*)

Curt Wild, founder of the influential garage band, The Rats –

DISSOLVE TO:

EXT. WOODS – MICHIGAN – NIGHT – 1946

Dark hand-held glimpses of animals, moving in pack, close to camera.

40

CECIL
(*voice-over*)
– came from the aluminium trailer parks of Michigan –
though rock folklore claims far more primitive origins.

EXT. TRAILER PARK – MICHIGAN – NIGHT – 1946

Long shot of a luminous silver trailer home.

*[A pack of black wolves leave a bundle at the door and saunter
off, looking back as they go. We hear a baby's cries and the door
opens.

A handsome white trash family peer out.

FAST BACK TO:]

EXT. OUTDOOR CONCERT – STAGE – NIGHT – 1971

CLOSE ON *Curt as he lifts a huge jar of gold glitter into the air and
begins slowly to shower himself, top to bottom, with the sparkling
substance.*

Intercut between Curt's glitter rain and the following shots, each in slight
SLOW MOTION:

Brian, his attention rapt. Rack to Cecil, behind him, noticing.

TRACKING *over the audience, tightening in waves. They turn restless
and noisy, fighting among themselves, throwing things.*

Curt responds by camping it up and blowing kisses at his perpetrators.

CECIL
(*voice-over*)
According to legend, when Curt was fourteen –

Briefly:

EXT. TRAILER HOME – MICHIGAN – DAY – 1960

Curt's half-naked Brother and Sis wrestle in the backyard, grabbing

*Cut from completed film.

41

each other's voluptuous bodies – and all for the benefit of fourteen-year-old Curt, who sits watching.

> CECIL
> (*voice-over*)

– he was discovered by his mother in the family loo, at the 'service' of his older brother –

FAST RETURN TO:

EXT. OUTDOOR CONCERT – STAGE – NIGHT – 1971

Curt turns around, drops his pants and moons the audience.

> CECIL
> (*voice-over*)

– and promptly shipped off for eighteen months of electric shock treatment.

The audience roars through.

CUT TO:

INT. WAYNE COUNTY SANITARIUM – MICHIGAN – DAY – 1960

Doors swing open to the psych ward and we whisk through.

> RECORDED VOICE

You are now entering Wayne County. Please proceed to ground floor Reception.

Curt, strapped down to the traveling gurney, hooked up with electrodes, comes to a sudden halt. He looks up at:

His family (Ma, Pa, Brother and Sis), all looking down at him. Ma clutches a Bible.

> CECIL
> (*voice-over*)

The doctors guaranteed the treatment would fry the fairy clean out of him.

Curt's Brother gives him a wink.

But all it did was make him bonkers –

The Doctor flips the switch.

Curt leaps into the air in a contorted frenzy.

EXT. OUTDOOR CONCERT – STAGE – NIGHT – 1971

> CECIL
> (*voice-over*)
– every time he heard electric guitar.

The audience roars in delirium. Someone throws a paper torch on to the stage and all the oil goes up.

Surrounded in flames, Curt shrieks victoriously, glaring at the audience. All at once he goes running off the edge of the stage, leaping into the swarm of spectators.

SUDDEN CUT TO:

EXT. PARK HILLSIDE – SUNRISE – 1971

Quiet. Brian looks out at the dawn.

He sits with Mandy on a grassy hill, near the concert grounds.

> BRIAN
> (*quietly*)
They despised him.

Cecil's eyes open from half-sleep, leaning against a nearby tree.

> MANDY
> (*also quietly*)
Yeah. But when you're abused like that . . . you know you've touched the stars.

CLOSE ON *Brian against nectarine skies.*

> BRIAN
I know. I just –

Mandy looks at him.

> (*softly, as if to himself*)
– wish it'd been me.

Wish I'd thought of it.

Quiet waves of music: Mandy is touched by his confession.

MANDY
(*tenderly*)
You will, luv. You will.

ZOOM IN *as Brian turns. He looks at her as an upbeat glam song begins ('The Ballad of Maxwell Demon'/Shudder to Think), the first to tell the story of a tragic space hero named Maxwell Demon.*

CUT TO:

IRIS OUT TO:

LONDON ROOFTOPS – DUSK – PAINTED SET

In a Disney CLOSE-UP, *Curt Wild (dressed as a Satyr) winks to camera, and turns.* ZOOM OUT *as he leaps into a chimney-stack against a painted backdrop.*

The ZOOM *continues, revealing the rooftop vista in a gilded frame and hanging in an empty white space.*

INT. WHITE SET

The ZOOM OUT *is joined by a* TRACK *which reveals Brian, dressed as a pink and blue nineteenth-century dandy, viewing the painting behind a red velvet rope. When revealed, he turns to camera and starts to sing.*

In CLOSE-UP *he plucks the pink rosebud from his lapel and sings a verse of the song to it. It blooms in his hands.*

He steps back from the painting and begins to 'mime-walk' on, staying in place while the view in the painting passes.

Swish to:

EXTREME CLOSE-UP *of two fingers placing a tiny Victorian dollhouse on a white pedestal. Fast* ZOOM OUT *reveals Brian standing beside the pedestal, now full-size. He leans over and peers inside.*

INT. DOLLHOUSE DRAWING ROOM – SET

Through a veil of sequined gauze, a shimmering creature looks up. It's Brian, dressed as the green alien, not unlike the image of Curt on the rooftop, but clean and sparkly. We follow as he creeps past the mist of gauze into the light of the room. Suddenly he jolts.

One enormous eye (Brian's) glares through the window.

Brian the alien slithers across the black and white check floors of the elegant drawing room and disappears behind a door.

INT. DOLLHOUSE BEDROOM – SET

Brian the alien surprises an inflatable doll husband and wife in bed whose arms fly up when they see him.

EXTREME CLOSE-UP: *he gives a look to camera.*

In a hi-speed master (à la Clockwork Orange*) Brian rapes the wife doll and then the husband.*

CLOSE ON: *Brian's eyes, blinking through the bedroom window.*

As the song describes Maxwell Demon's rise to stardom we intercut Brian's eye blinking through the window with the following vignettes in COLLAGE ANIMATION:

INT. WHITE SET

EXTREME CLOSE-UP *of a long match being struck and lighting a cigarette. Fast* ZOOM OUT *reveals life-size Brian inhaling from an enormous cigarette holder as he tosses the matchstick on to the dollhouse. It goes up in smoke.*

INT. DOLLHOUSE – SET

Through the flames, Brian the alien is grinning, jamming on his guitar.

FAST CUT TO:

INT. RECORD STUDIO – CONFERENCE ARENA – DAY – 1972

Music holds on a row of faceless Execs (seen previously in the 'Imaginary Theatre') facing camera in smoky darkness. (One of them

we now recognize as Arthur's boss, Lou.) We hear the sound of one
person clapping. Everyone looks over. Swish pan to:

Jerry Devine (mid-thirties), seated alone with a cigar. He wears an
Italian 'fro' with fat mutton chops.

> DEVINE
> *(extending his hand)*

Nice stuff.

Brian's gloved hand shakes it. Zoom-out reveals him in a three-piece
business suit.

> BRIAN

Thanks.

> DEVINE

Devine. Jerry Devine. Personal management. I'm interested.

> BRIAN

Oh, well – *thank* you – but I'm afraid I already have
management. He's –

Cecil smiles and waves from his seat.

DEVINE

Not in my opinion.

Cecil's eyes bulge. 'A quiet swell of music' begins beneath (the intro to 'The Whole Shebang'/Grant Lee Philips).

The truth is you have talent. That's plain. But it doesn't really matter what a man does in his life. All that really matters in the end is the legend that grows up around him. Now today you're a talented singer. That's fine. But I could make you a star.

CECIL
(standing, angrily)
And just how do you propose to do that?

DEVINE

I will tell you, sir . . .

Devine pushes up a shirt sleeve and places his elbow on the railing before him, his other hand joustingly on his hip.

When you pin me.

Murmurs from the crowd as Cecil bolts up from his chair.

CECIL

Well I have never in all my life –

Cecil looks around helplessly for defense.

Everyone just stares at him, evil music rising softly. Zoom in to Brian, furthest away, who looks down.

CLOSE ON *Cecil, his heart broken. Fast track to Devine, poised in the spotlight behind him.*

DEVINE

May the best man win?

We punch into the chorus of 'The Whole Shebang'.

CUT TO:

INT. TV STUDIO – NIGHT – 1972

Brian performs the song on Top of the Pops, *his entire band dressed in gold lamé.*

> BBC VOICE
> (*off-screen*)
> Earlier tonight on the popular chart show *Top of the Pops*, newcomer Brian Slade performed his hit single 'The Whole Shebang' –

PULL OUT TO REVEAL:

INT. LONDON PUB – EVENING – 1972

TRACK *along the line of blokes at the bar, staring up at the telly.*

> BBC VOICE
> – dressed in gold lamé and wearing glitter eye make-up. A spokesman for the show, known for showcasing pop's brightest stars, says they've been deluged with calls all evening.

TRACK *ends on Cecil, sitting over a cocktail in the corner. He watches the broadcast solemnly.*

CECIL
(*pre-lap*[†])

The next day every schoolgirl in London was wearing glitter eye make-up. And I was out of a bleeding job.

CUT TO:

INT. CITY HOSPITAL – NEW YORK – DAY –1984

Cecil shakes his head with a distant smile.

CECIL

And that, as they say, was that. I would not hear another word from Brian – or any of them for that matter – ever again.

ARTHUR

Do you have any idea what ultimately happened to him? Where he is today?

Cecil just shrugs.

CECIL

Last I heard he'd returned to Birmingham, but this was – three years ago? Four? No, I'm afraid I can't help you there. Looks as if it may be unavoidable.

ARTHUR

What's that.

CECIL

The ex, I'm afraid. But then every story needs a contrary opinion, and with Mandy you're guaranteed excesses of both.

FAST CUT TO:

*[EXT./INT. DIVE CLUB – NEW YORK – LATE DAY – 1984

A bolt of music strikes a dirty marquee: 'APPEARING NITELY – THE DIVINE MISS MANDY SLADE'.

The bar's front door opens and we enter the crumbling nightclub,

[†]Pre-lap: Dialogue from the ensuing scene heard before the cut.
*Cut from completed film.

49

approaching a lone figure bent over a table, the only person in sight.
Suddenly a large Bartender, Latino, steps into frame, blocking our way.

> BARTENDER
> Hey – fellah, we're not open – Hey!

> ARTHUR
> I'm from the *Herald?*

> BARTENDER
> I don't care if you're from Planet X – We still don't open till
> seven –

> ARTHUR
> Mandy Slade told me to meet her here at four. I'm a little
> late, I'm sorry –

> BARTENDER
> (*softly*)
> Mandy did?

The music suddenly softens.

> ARTHUR
> Yes.

He slowly turns, looking back over his shoulder: and there she sits.

> BARTENDER
> Man? . . .]

We resume our approach past the Bartender.

Arthur nears her, feeling a pang of ill ease.

> ARTHUR
> Miss Slade?

Mandy slowly lifts her head and squints up at him.

> MANDY
> Yeah?

> ARTHUR
> I'm Arthur Stuart – from the *Herald?* We spoke on the phone?

She looks at him blankly.

> I'm sorry I'm a bit late. I really just have a few questions I
> wanted to ask. It shouldn't take long.

Nothing.

> Do you mind if I – sit down?

MANDY

> It's a free country. Sort of.

Arthur sits.

*The Bartender stands staring at Arthur as Mandy sits staring into her
drink.*

ARTHUR

> What're you having?

She looks up at him.

MANDY

> You, looks like.

Arthur smiles.

(quietly)
Scotch. Rocks.

ARTHUR
(to Bartender)
Make that two.

The Bartender drags off, mumbling.

MANDY
Gee. You must be after some damn exclusive copy.

ARTHUR
It's a piece on Brian Slade?

MANDY
(dryly sarcastic)
No kidding. What – sort of a memory jog kind of thing?

ARTHUR
Well . . . You see, it's been ten years since the whole fake
shooting incident –

MANDY
And what a fake it was! Tricking us all in the end with such
an authentic demise.

ARTHUR

His career, you mean?

CLOSE ON *Mandy, looking up from her drink. She can't suppress a smirk, which spreads to a snicker.*

I mean, do you have any idea what happened to him, where he is today?

MANDY

Can't you just, you know, run him through the files? Punch in the name?

ARTHUR

Not exactly.

Mandy starts opening up a fresh pack of cigarettes.

MANDY

Because, honestly darling, I haven't spoken with Mr Slade in – seven years, at least.

ARTHUR

Seven years. Wow.

MANDY

Wow. At least – Smoke?

ARTHUR

No. Thanks.

MANDY

No, right after everything crashed we – we split . . . And Brian, he just –

She lights a cigarette and takes a drag.

– became someone else.

She turns to Arthur and exhales.

(*a distant smile*)
But then he always was.

The opulent strains of Mahler's Sixth Symphony begin over

DISSOLVE TO:

EXT. SOMBRERO CLUB – NEW YEAR'S EVE – NIGHT – 1969

We follow an elegantly dressed couple through a boisterous wind as they approach the doors of the club. Leaves swirl through the air and the man's cape billows as the doors of the club swing open. The teenage doorman, Cooper, greets the couple and they enter, descending the stairs to the club below. Inside the chandelier swings with the wind.

Then Cooper, the doorman, turns to camera:

> COOPER
> That'll be ten bob to you, mate.

Off-screen a hand delivers the money.

REVERSE ANGLE *reveals Brian, aged twenty-one, looking every inch the London hippie with a mass of blond curls and jewelry. He gives Cooper a quick once-over before stepping into the club. We follow as 'Get in the Groove' by the Mighty Hannibal rises.*

INT. SOMBRERO CLUB – NEW YEAR'S EVE – NIGHT – 1969

Brian descends through pink and purple light, taking it all in. A swirl of color as we pan across the room to Mandy, close, laughing and smoking with friends.

A Drag-Queen is standing on stage conducting the crowds. Behind her a bright banner reads: 'WELCOME TO THE SEVENTIES!'

In the corner, glowing in colored lights, a light-up dance floor is pumping with dance.

Mandy glows in a bright green unisex one-piece. Then all at once she spots him.

Brian, scanning the club, catches sight of her.

Mandy quickly returns to her friends, laughing, smoking.

Brian watches.

MANDY
(*voice-over*)
It was New Year's Eve 1969: the start of a new decade, –

Brian watches Mandy amid a flood of hugs and kisses.

– and everywhere you went there was this sense of the future,
the feeling in the air that anything was possible.

*A sudden crash of cymbals and dimming of lights directs everyone's
attention to the club's entrance upstairs.*

A spotlight is spun around, followed by a luxurious swish pan to:

*The top of the curving staircase. There, aglow in shimmering pastels,
Jack Fairy, the Sombrero's reigning star, is making his entrance. He
nods regally and begins to descend, flanked by an equally studded
entourage: Micki, a pretty boy in perfect Marilyn drag, Angel, a buxom
brunette in feathers, and Freddi, the group stylist, in satin breeches and
stockings. A quiet swirl of music accompanies.*

See, Jack Fairy had also come to London in the swinging
sixties.

DISSOLVE TO:

INT. POSH HOTEL LOBBY – EVENING – 1967

A black silk scarf falling to the floor (music continuing).

*A delicate hand with nails of black enamel and a menagerie of rings
reaches for the scarf. We follow it up past the lithe, velvety figure of Jack
Fairy, who wraps the scarf elegantly around his neck and fastens it with
the emerald pin.*

MANDY
(*voice-over*)
And on winding roads, in crowded clubs and hotel bars – this
shipwreck of the streets stirred the daydreams of London
trash and glamor, his cigarette tracing a ladder to the stars.

EXTREME CLOSE-UP *of Jack opening a small compact. Zoom into
mirror where three Waiters are reflected.*

CLOSE ON *their mouths, each whispering a word in turn:*

Maricon, épicène, sexe douteux . . .

Suddenly Jack glances up.

ZOOM IN *to a small balcony where the Businessman stands looking over.*

Jack looks up, closing his compact and standing.

Everyone in the lavishly decorated nineteenth-century hotel lobby stares as Jack walks proudly across the room.

A Gentleman in the foreground turns to camera and confides:

GENTLEMAN
Le Vice Anglais . . .

FAST CUT TO:

INT. SOMBRERO CLUB – NEW YEAR'S EVE – NIGHT – 1969

CLOSE ON *someone kissing Jack's hand. Fast* ZOOM OUT *to:*

Jack, soft and slightly SLOW MOTION, *engulfed at the foot of the stairs. A sexy Hustler, dressed as a 1930s sailor, finishes kissing his hand and Cooper presents him with a long-stemmed rose. But there is an undertow: the eerie intro to 'Ladytron'/Roxy Music begins to rise.*

MANDY
(*voice-over*)
I needn't mention how essential dreaming is to the character of the rock star.

Brian, very CLOSE. *Suddenly someone shrieks, breaking the spell. Mandy bursts through bodies with open arms.*

Jack, darling!

FAST CUT TO:

INT. DIVE CLUB – NEW YORK – DAY – 1984

Mandy, CLOSE.

MANDY

Jack was truly the first of his kind. A true original, everyone
stole from Jack.

FAST RETURN.

INT. SOMBRERO CLUB – NEW YEAR'S EVE – NIGHT – 1969

*Mandy has her arms around Jack and her tongue down his throat. He
pulls away and she laughs, pulling him into the club. As she turns, she
spots:*

Brian – FAST ZOOM IN *– still staring through the crowds. Closer on
Mandy, as Jack looks over as well, also seeing him.*

Brian, CLOSE, *music building. He spots the emerald pin, dangling from
Jack's ear. We hear*

MANDY
(*voice-over*)

But from the moment Brian Slade stepped into our lives,
nothing would ever be the same.

DISSOLVE TO:

INT. SOMBRERO CLUB – NEW YEAR'S EVE – NIGHT – 1969

Brian's face slowly approaching, through the crowds.

MANDY
(*voice-over*)

It was his nature.

Brian's voice is heard, singing with the music:

BRIAN
(*singing; off-screen*)

You've got me girl on the runaround,
runaround/Got me all around town
You've got me girl on the runaround
And it's getting me down, getting me down

We TRACK (*slight* SLOW MOTION) *through bodies to where Mandy stands dancing/chatting with Jack and company. Suddenly she turns and sees:*

Brian approaching. The lights and set begin to change: the dancing slows and everything but Mandy and Brian dim and recede.

Brian takes Mandy's hand and instantly they are surrounded by a cool

*midnight snowfall. The club has vanished into the surrounding
darkness, and as he begins to sing to her, we begin a slow* TRACK
around them.

> BRIAN
> (*singing*)
> Lady/If you want to find a lover
> Then you look no further
> For I'm gonna be your only
> Searching/At the start of the season
> And my only reason/Is that I'll get you

The song breaks into a driving bridge as we:

CUT TO:

INT. SOMBRERO CLUB – NEW YEAR'S EVE – LATER –1969

*Mandy, in the midst of the teaming dance floor, turns to Brian,
standing opposite (lights and action having returned to normal).*

> BRIAN
> (*shouting over the music*)
> Do you jive?

Mandy nods, smiling, and they start to dance.

FAST DISSOLVE TO:

INT. MANDY'S BEDROOM – NIGHT – 1970

*Music continues through a brief sixties-style montage (much double
exposure, focus racking, etc.). Mandy and Brian make love like two
amphibious creatures in Mandy's candle-lit room.*

*The erotic tone turns sinister as other-worldly projections fall across their
bodies, indistinguishable in the flickering light. [Sequence will be shot
through water, with the projections of moonlit water sparkling over their
bodies.]*

For a moment Brian appears to be turning amphibious.

Mandy closes her eyes.

EXT. FOREST — NIGHT — 1970

CLOSE ON *a raven, blinking in the cool moonlight. We descend through a snarl of black branches to a moonlit forest where Brian resumes his tender serenade.*

> BRIAN
> (*singing*)
> I'll find some way of connection
> Hiding my intention
> Then I'll move up close to you

TRACK *continues into Brian's face, shimmery with sweat.*

> I'll use you and I'll confuse you
> And then I'll lose you
> But still you won't suspect me

He kisses her.

> MANDY
> (*voice-over*)
> So I married him.

FAST CUT TO:

INT. SOMBRERO CLUB — MEN'S LAVATORY — NEW YEAR'S EVE — 1969

The flutter of an eyelash (Jack's) thick with mascara.

We hear a door open, sounds pouring in. Jack's eyes flash over.

Fast rack to Brian, standing near the door, reflected in the mirror. Quiet music begins.

A series of CLOSE, DISSOLVING SHOTS:

Jack resumes touching up his face in the mirror as Brian slowly approaches.

Jack's eyes meet Brian's in the mirror.

Brian stops at the mirror, turning from Jack's reflection to Jack. He kisses him hotly on the mouth and withdraws.

60

Jack stares into Brian's eyes. He returns the kiss. Brian presses into him.

Suddenly – the door opens.

Jack turns.

Brian is gone.

FADE TO BLACK.

T-Rex's 'Cosmic Dancer' begins in darkness.

FAST CUT TO:

INT. MANDY'S BEDROOM – NIGHT – 1972

Slow circle around Mandy and Brian as she finishes painting his face: the lids of his eyes are metallic green (eyebrows shaven), his cheeks a silver-pink blush, his lips a frosty magenta, matching the color of his newly cropped hair.

>MANDY
>Times, places, people. They're all speeding up. So to cope with this evolutionary paranoia strange people are chosen who through their art can move progress more quickly.

Brian looks up.

Mandy holds his glance.

>(*voice-over*)
>It was the most stimulating and reflective period of our marriage.

He turns and looks at himself in the mirror.

RACK/DISSOLVE TO:

INT. SOMBRERO CLUB – MEN'S ROOM – NEW YEAR'S EVE – 1969

Jack in the mirror feels for his earring and realizes the emerald pin is gone. He looks down at his finger.

There's a drop of blood.

61

Through rising music ('We Are the Boys'/Pulp) we hear:

BBC

(pre-lap)

Thank you and welcome, pop pickers, to *Pick of the Pops*. I'm
Davy Rocket and we have a very special show for you today,
dedicated to one of pop's blazing new talents, and one who's
been holding a virtual reign over the British charts for a
startling eighteen-month record-span. Ladies and gentlemen,
I give you the incomparable Brian Slade – or should I say,
Maxwell Demon?

Cheers spill over.

FAST CUT TO:

INT. GALA RECEPTION HALL – LONDON – NIGHT – 1972

An explosion of flash bulbs over a sweep of music.

*Brian appears through the shimmer, ablaze in white light. He wears the
emerald pin on a red velvet choker. Below, a small ocean of press
(Reporters, Photographers) are shouting 'Brian! Brian!'*

REPORTER 1

Brian! Why the make-up?

BRIAN

Why? Because rock and roll's a prostitute! It should be tarted
up! Performed! The music is the mask, while I, in my chiffon
and taff – *well* –

(quite camp)

– varda the message!

INT. STUART LIVING ROOM – SUBURBAN MANCHESTER –
EVENING – 1972

Teenage Arthur sits on the floor glued to the telly.

*His Mother and Father sit behind him (exactly as we last saw them),
watching without expression.*

62

REPORTER 2
(*on TV*)

What about your fans? Aren't they likely to – get the wrong
impression?

BRIAN
(*on TV*)

And which wrong impression is that?

Brian snickers.

REPORTER 2
(*on TV*)

That you're a blinking fruit!

On-screen there is uneasy laughter and a SHAKY PAN *to the press
gallery.*

VERY CLOSE ON *Arthur, breathing in the electronic waves.*

BRIAN
(*on TV*)

Well thank you, sir, and no, it doesn't concern me in the
least.

*Arthur tries to peek at his parents without moving his head. Their faces
are stony.*

I should think that if people were to get that impression of
me, the one to which you so eloquently refer . . .

SLOW TRACK *into Brian on monitor.*

. . . it would not be a wrong impression in the slightest.

*Suddenly Arthur leaps in front of the set, shrieking at the top of his
lungs like a lunatic.*

ARTHUR

That is me! That is me! That that that is *me*!

CLOSE ON *TV.*

BRIAN
(*on TV*)

I mean, everyone knows most people are bisexual.

63

Arthur's Mother and Father are blank-faced, frozen solid.

Arthur looks back at them, back in front of the TV set (where he has remained).

                    REPORTER
                   (*off-screen*)
        I was –

BACK TO:

INT. GALA RECEPTION HALL – LONDON – EVENING – 1972

Shaky PAN *to another Reporter.*

                    REPORTER
                   (*off-screen*)
        – I was under the impression that you were married and living
        with your wife in North London –

Mandy looks around, anxiously.

Brian continues in the glare of lights.

                     BRIAN
        I *am* married, quite happily, in fact. I just happen to like boys
        as much as I like girls. And since my wife feels pretty much
        the same about such things . . .

Lights and TV cameras flash to Mandy, who wiggles her tongue at Brian.

        . . . I should think we've been able to make a fairly decent go
        of it up to now.

The audience, frozen in utter perplexity.

Mandy looks up at Brian, as the distant piano opening to 'Virginia Plain'/Roxy Music is heard.

[**Note:** the several scenes following which accompany 'Virginia Plain' should be played with tremendous speed and energy.]

                    MANDY
                  (*voice-over*)
        For the first time in Brian's life, he was simply telling it like it

                        64

was. Did he realize what he'd actually *done*? How could he have? I mean today, there'd be fighting in the streets. But in 1972 . . .

Brian winks at Mandy before – complete pandemonium.

. . . it was more like dancing.

VERY CLOSE ON: *Brian as we:*

DISSOLVE TO:

Fame montage:

INT. NEWSPAPERS (IN BLACK AND WHITE) – SET – 1972

Dropped into frame, their headlines read:

A STAR IS BORN – AND HE TWINKLES!
GAY STUNT AT SLADE SHOW
ALL THAT GLITTERS – IS GAY!

INT. RECORD STUDIO – CONFERENCE ARENA – DAY – 1972

Camera speeds past a Busby Berkeley-style row of proffered contracts and lands on the final one – the most elegantly drawn.

Swoop out from Jerry Devine and Cecil Drake arm-wrestling; it ends as Devine wins and stands, the champion. Crowds cheer. He is thrown a huge bouquet.

Brief photo-flash: Brian, nude in Devine's arms, covered in roses.

EXT. HIGHWAY – ENGLAND – DAY – 1972

Brian and his flashy entourage soar along the countryside in two convertible limousines, scarves sailing in the wind.

EXT. AIRPORT RUNWAY – DAY – 1972

Brian and company scramble on to the stairway of a chartered plane.

EXT. ENGLISH GARDEN – DAY – 1972

Brian and Mandy lounge in sunglasses.

We hear:

DEVINE
(*off-screen*)

That man out there in the white suit is the biggest thing to come out of England since sliced Beatles. Outside this country – nobody knows who the hell he is. You people, you're going to change all that.

FAST ZOOM OUT *reveals Devine in the foreground. He faces camera, addressing his newly formed staff.*

TRACK *past faces we've seen before – Jack Fairy's old entourage: Angel, Micki, Freddi, and Sombero Club doorboy Cooper.*

Now each of you are actors. It's up to you to transform the image of pop singer Brian Slade into space-age fuckin' superstar Maxwell Demon. Nothing fantastic about it. Why? Because the secret of becoming a star is in knowing how to behave as one.

COOPER
(*a distorted Mickey Rooney voice*)

Hey kids, let's put on a show!

Disturbingly CLOSE ON *Devine:*

Precisely.

EXT. ENGLISH GARDEN – DAY – 1972

CLOSE ON *Jack Fairy in white face, gazing to camera. Rapid zoom out reveals him posing as a statue of Saint Sebastian.*

TRACK OUT *from* CLOSE-UP *of Brian being aggressively made up, sprayed and varnished by Freddi and company. Brian is dressed in a white satin three-piece, posing for photos with his band in the eighteenth-century statue garden. The sequence has the feel of a silent screen comedy, with Devine as director in jodhpurs and boots, commanding the company of Photographers and Crew. Equipment and dress is strictly twenties.*

When Devine shouts 'action', the klatch of Photographers explode into shots, their cameras flashing like machine-guns.

Brian is riddled with tiny wounds. Devine yells 'Cut!' furiously.

In a series of fast-cutting shots, Brian continues to be 'shot' in various poses and costumes, each time trying to conceal the pain and blood-stains.

End on a final, classic shot. Fast ZOOM OUT *reveals the photo hanging on a wall in the brand-new Bijou Music offices:*

INT. BIJOU OFFICES – DAY – 1972

Camera continues through the Bijou offices as the newly assembled staff perform their respective roles with musical comedy flair (song continuing throughout).

We sail past Micki, the glamorous receptionist, rehearsing various company greetings.

                    MICKI
Bijou Music and Associates, good afternoon . . . Bijou, may I help you? . . . Bijou, hello? . . .

We pass Angel, press attaché, dressed in large black and white checks and a matching pillbox hat. Her walls are covered with glamor

*magazines from the thirties and forties, and everything on her desk is
cherry red: phone, typewriter, telexes, etc.*

ANGEL

Slade . . . Brian Slade . . . Well, darling, only the biggest
thing to hit rock since the pilgrims! . . .

Next, they pass Devine in his elevated office.

*Manager Jerry Devine, is perched behind his desk in wide lapels and
clashing patterns, operatic on the phone.*

DEVINE

I *know* it's unprecedented, I know it's unorthodox, but, sir, if
you want Brian Slade, those are the terms, you may take them
or leave them –

Freddi suddenly pops out, addressing camera.

FREDDI

Yes?

SWISH *360-degrees to Shannon Hazelbourne, a dowdy teenager, who
responds automatically.*

SHANNON

I'm Shannon Hazelbourne.

68

Who?

SHANNON
I rang up about the position?

FREDDI
The what?

SHANNON
The *position.*
   (*holding up a clipping*)
Assistant Clerical Aid?

FREDDI
Oh *right!* The position! Brilliant! Follow me.

Shannon tries to keep up with Freddi who whizzes into the wardrobe room.

INT. WARDROBE – DAY – 1972

Brian's (all-hetero) band – Trevor, Reg and Harley – stand frozen in the mirror.

MANDY
(*off-screen*)
Crash! Zounds.

FAST ZOOM OUT *reveals them in their new, wildly effeminate stage costumes. Mandy beams as Freddi whizzes by.*

TREVOR
Fuckin' Ada – you're *gorgeous* –

MANDY
Aren't they?

Harley looks mournfully at Trevor. Trevor puts his arm around him tenderly.

We hear:

FREDDI
(*off-screen*)

Now, Shannon – I realize, of course, your expertise is in the clerical arts, but I was wondering if by any chance you've ever worked in wardrobe?

SWISH *to Shannon, standing dumbstruck.*

. . . either professionally or –

SHANNON

No, never.

FREDDI

Fantastic. I think that's everything.
(*extends his hand*)

SHANNON
(*shaking it, absently*)

But I – I said *didn't* –

Freddie walks into the main office.

INT. BIJOU OFFICES – DAY – 1972

FREDDIE
(*announcing to the room*)

Everybody?

Everyone looks over.

I'd like to introduce you to our lovely new Wardrobe Mistress – umm . . .

SHANNON

Shannon.

FREDDI

Shannon.

Everyone smiles, claps or says: 'Hello Shannon'. Mandy suddenly looks over toward Devine's office.

We hear:

DEVINE
(*off-screen*)
Excellent! Yes, Mr Weinberg! Thank you very much indeed.
Cheers!

Mighty SWISH *to:*

Devine slams down phone. Fast pan up to his face, standing victoriously.

Extraordinary!

Everyone turns.

MANDY
What, Jerry – *what*?

DEVINE
So! Tell me, Master Demon . . .

TRACK IN *to the back of a large chair from which Brian reveals himself, turning to Devine.*

Who is it you most fancy meeting – in *America*?

Everyone bursts into cheers. TRACK OUT *as Mandy and Cooper escort Devine from his desk, revealing the Bijou office to be a network of adjoining offices, art deco style. Brian remains alone.*

MICKI
Yipes.

COOPER
(*with a broad American accent*)
American?

ANGEL
Bravo, Jerry!

MANDY
Garbo, Brian – pleeeease!

ANGEL
Brando for me.

MICKI
Einstein!

COOPER

Sorry, chickee, he's dead.

MICKI

Jerry said anyone!

Brian turns to the group. Mandy spots him.

MANDY

Brian – *who*?

BRIAN

I guess . . .

Devine turns to him.

DEVINE

Yes, Brian?

Song finishes with 'What's her name? Virginia Plain.'
Silence on Brian.

BRIAN
(*quietly*)

Curt Wild.

DEVINE

What?

BRIAN
(*awkward, first time yet*)
Curt Wild. I want to meet Curt Wild.

CLOSE ON. *Mandy, looking at him.*

Slam into Guitar intro ('Personality Crisis'/New York Dolls).

MANDY
(*voice-over*)
And meet Curt Wild we did.

CUT TO:

INT. MAX'S KANSAS CITY – NEW YORK – NIGHT – 1973

Brian and Mandy are walking into the dark, narrow club, followed by Devine, Angel, Freddi and Trevor.

On stage, Polly Small, a tough girl singer in a black leather jump suit, belts out a gendy-bendy Beatles cover. She's backed by a gloriously trashy, New York-style glam band.

Rodney, a British rep for the label, leads them to a table in the back.

The black-clad Hipster Crowd eyes the colorful Brits as they pass.

Rodney stops for a moment and looks around the room.

Brian looks around as well, expectant and anxious, taking it all in. Mandy leans over, pointing out someone.

Andy Warhol stands in the back in the midst of a small entourage. Swish to: James Dean, standing in another corner. Swish to: Marilyn Monroe, seated at the bar.

RODNEY
(*off-screen*)
There he is.

Brian looks over to Rodney who points, music shimmering.

Dark figures clear frame as we track in to the darkest corner of the club. Reveal a shadowy figure slumped over a table.

CLOSE ON *Brian, following Rodney, arriving. Somewhere behind the music we hear:*

Mr Wild . . . Mr *Wild*?

Curt lifts up his head, squinting up at Rodney. He sits between a beautiful pair of boy and girl Teenage Twins.

CURT

Yeah?

RODNEY

I'm Rodney – from Electra? I have Brian Slade here from England who just wanted to pop over, say hello –

BRIAN

I just wanted to say . . . I think your music is tops – smashing, really – best of the lot.

Curt looks up at him in a junkie blur.

CURT

Smashing, top hole, jolly old –

Curt's eyes roll up into his head and he passes out on the table.

Brian in diffused CLOSE-UP *as 'Slaughter on 10th Avenue'/Mick Ronson begins with dramatic flourish.*

He has fallen in love.

CUT TO:

INT. HOTEL MEZZANINE – AFTERNOON – 1973

Pan over guests seated for tea at a posh New York hotel.

MANDY
(voice-over)

Now at that time, Curt Wild was between management, and Brian knew this, of course, and urged Devine to pursue the situation.

We settle on a corner table where Brian and Devine sit with Curt, a black smudge against the crimson and gold interior.

> DEVINE
> And so if, in that probability, an interest arose in which Brian would serve in some capacity *on* a future project – possibly, though not exclusively, as *producer* of that project – we're taking our cue from you here, Curt – how might that scenario – purely hypothetically, of course – how might that scenario strike you at this juncture?

Silence as Curt looks back at them with the innocence of a drowned rat.

> BRIAN
> What Jerry's trying to say is do you want to come to London to cut a record?

> CURT
> Oh yeah – cool.

> DEVINE
> Very *good.*

> BRIAN
> But how can we *help* you. You must tell us. What do you *need?*

Under the table Devine kicks Brian in the shin. Curt thinks for a moment, then smiles:

> CURT
> Everything.

Brian smiles.

> See, heroin was my mainman. But I'm on the methadone. I'm finally getting my act together. I mean . . . You say you wanna help? I say *far out.*
> > (*to Brian, softly*)
> *You* can be my mainman.

CLOSE ON *Brian through diffusion, watching Curt. There are tiny hearts in his eyes.*

> MANDY
> (*voice-over*)
It was pretty clear what was happening. It happens every day.
But for the *world* to think it was happening, well . . .

Pan to Devine, in foreground, tiny dollar signs in his eyes.

That was Jerry's particular genius.

'Satellite of Love'/Lou Reed begins:

CUT TO:

Montage of newsreel-style footage:

EXT. BRIAN'S GARDEN – DAY – 1973

HANDHELD TELEPHOTO *shots into Brian's back garden: Brian and
Curt stroll with champagne, eventually catching sight of the camera.*

> MANDY
> (*voice-over*)
Right away he started promoting the two of them like a pair of
forties starlets on the swoon – a Tracy and Hepburn for the
seventies.

Song continues.

EXT. MOVIE PALACE – NIGHT – 1973

*Limousine doors open and Brian and Curt, dressed to the nines, pile
out. They are instantly obliterated by floodlights and camera flashes as
they stumble up the red carpet, waving to fans like a pair of drunken
screen stars.*

CUT TO:

EXT. CARNIVAL – SET – DUSK – 1973

*Curt and Brian ride in neighboring rockets on the Space Spinner ride,
reeling over the candy-colored lights of a traveling carnival.* TRACK-IN
*as Curt lip-syncs to the song and Brian sings the backing arpeggios, his
rocket passing Curt's.*

Behind them, the lights of the carnival recede. They are flying away.

Pan up to the starry sky as the music becomes tender ('Diamond Meadows'/T-Rex).

DREAMY DISSOLVE TO:

INT. LITTLE GIRL'S ROOM – NIGHT – 1973

PAN PAST *a forty-five spinning on a plastic turntable, and come to rest on the soft, lamp-lit* CLOSE-UP *of a Brian Slade doll.*

Opposite, a Curt Wild doll stands against a deluxe pop show backdrop. A gentle love scene is being played out by the hands and off-screen voices of two young English Girls. The scene is shot romantically, with soft lighting and heavy diffusion.

> CURT DOLL
> My career was on the skids, mate. And you fished me out o' the muck. You got me back on my feet, you did.

> BRIAN DOLL
> It was nothing, chum. I wanted to help you make more of that far-out sound. I love your music, my son, and I love –

The Brian doll turns away. The Curt doll walks up to him from behind.

> CURT DOLL
> (*softly*)
> You don't have to say it, mate.

The dolls turn toward each other and embrace. They slowly, tenderly go down to the floor.

CUT TO:

INT. ST FRANCIS HOTEL – NEW YORK – LATE AFTERNOON – 1973

Thirties-style Singer crooning to camera, pink-cheeked with patent-leather style hair ('Bitters End'/Roxy Music):

Three pencil-mustached back-ups, the Champagne Chorus, lean in and sing.

TRACK OUT *to reveal the singers amid Bijou's deliriously posh press soirée. Dressed for a masked ball, Brian and company lounge and pose for reporters, all elegantly assembled in a gilded banquet room.*

Behind a white feather mask, the princely Brian holds court on a gold
settee, supported by a den of beautiful Bisexuals. He holds a mask of
himself on a stick. We see Curt Wild, Jerry Devine, Micki, Angel,
Cooper, Freddi, Shannon, Trevor – and Mandy playing hostess.
Everyone is dressed in cream-and-gold velvet and satin, some of the men
in breeches and white stockings. A touch of Louis XIV permeates the
room. Reporters, on the other hand, are a dark cluster of suits.

The song continues as each 'actor' answers questions in quoted texts,
punctuated by slightly bruising CAMERA FLASHES.

DEVINE

Every great century that produces art is, so far, an artificial
century, and the work that seems the most natural and simple
of its time is always the result of the most self-conscious
effort.

Micki, dressed like Marilyn Monroe as Marie Antoinette, sits as Angel,
in long gold fall, brushes his hair.

MICKI
(doing his best Marilyn)
I am not really myself except in the midst of elegant crowds,

80

at the heart of rich districts, or amid the sumptuous
ornamentation of palace hotels, an army of servants and a
plush carpet underfoot . . .

Mandy, luminous in platinum curls, puffs from a long cigarette holder.

> ### MANDY
> What is true about music is true about life: that beauty reveals
> everything because it expresses nothing.

*Freddie, dressed as a leopard-skin Mozart, wears an enormous boa
constrictor around his neck.*

> ### FREDDI
> The first duty in life is to assume a pose. What the second
> duty is no one has yet found out.

*A sudden fanfare and dimming of lights reveals the projected backdrop
of a stylized big top. A spotlight flashes on Brian, who catches a whip
and top hat thrown to him from the wings. Fast* ZOOM OUT *reveals
Reporter I in the foreground, reading from a large placard on a stand.*

> ### REPORTER I
> (*theatrically*)
> The Aesthete Gives Characteristically
> Cynical Evidence, Replete with Pointed
> Epigram and Startling Paradox, while
> Explaining His Views on Morality in Art.

*[Curt's head leans into foreground, unmasks itself and addresses
camera:

> ### CURT
> (*the classic aside*)
> Englisher and Englisher!]

SWISH PAN *to the klatch of Reporters, now perched in the rafters, shouting
out their questions to Brian. He answers in the style of a circus MC.*

> ### REPORTER I
> Brian! Maxwell Demon is the story of a space creature who
> becomes a rock and roll messiah, only to be destroyed by his

---

*Cut from completed film.

own enormity. Are you saying this is *your* destiny? Are *you* Maxwell Demon?

> BRIAN
>
> Man is least himself when he talks in his own person! Give him a mask and he'll tell you the truth!

We see Shannon holding cue cards for Brian. SWISH PAN *to Reporter 2, shouting out:*

> REPORTER 2
>
> Is it your belief that all dandies are homosexuals?

TILT DOWN *to Cooper, holding up cue cards for the press.*

> BRIAN
>
> Nothing makes one so vain as being told one is a sinner!

The stadium roars with laughter and applause.

> CURT
> (*off-screen*)
> Coming through! Coming through!

A spotlight spins around, illuminating.

Curt, squeezing through a throng of fans, balancing two glasses of champagne on a tray. There is clown music as he stumbles.

> REPORTER 3
>
> Tell us, Brian! Are the rumors true that you and Curt Wild have some sort of plans up your sleeve?

> BRIAN
>
> Oh, yes. Quite soon actually we plan to take over the world!

Hilarious laughter from the crowds – LOW ANGLE.

CLOSE ON *Brian: he wasn't joking. But to the rescue*

Curt arrives, miraculously unspilled.

> CURT
>
> Excuse me, fellas, while I raise my glass to the loveliest man in Europe!

The crowd 'Ahhhs' and Curt and Brian, smiling broadly, link arms for a toast, cameras flashing.

BRIAN
And they tell you it's not natural!

Violent laughter from the crowds quickly darkens and distorts. Lights dim as a shimmer of music rises.

FAST DISSOLVE TO:

Curt and Brian, eyelash close.

CURT
(*a whisper*)
The world is changed because you are made of ivory and gold. The curves of your lips rewrite history.

Curt kisses Brian hotly on the mouth. For several seconds all sound stops. Then:

Bang as camera flashes ignite the screen.

FAST DISSOLVE TO:

BLACK AND WHITE PHOTO — 1973

Curt kissing Brian — under the first slams of 'Babies on Fire'/Brian Eno.

CUT TO:

INT. CONCERT HALL — LONDON — NIGHT — 1973

Brian sings on-stage, glistening in sweat and a skintight strip tunic.

CLOSE.

Curt plays guitar. We see his fingers pressing the strings. Music continues through brief montage.

INT. MAGAZINE PRESS — DAY — 1973

We see editions of the 'kiss photo' being printed, cut and bound on machines. We see magazines boxed and loaded into trucks.

EXT. NEWSSTAND — DAY — 1973

Boxes are opened by vendors and put on display. Money is handed to vendors and magazines are handed back in exhange.

ARTHUR'S BEDROOM – SUBURBAN MANCHESTER – NIGHT – 1973

TRACK OUT *from the 'kiss photo' in Teenage Arthur's* Melody Maker *magazine.*

CLOSE ON *Arthur, lips moist, entranced.*

DISSOLVE TO:

INT. HOTEL SUITE – NEW YORK – NIGHT – 1973

A man's hand takes that of a woman's, leading her past flowing curtains to a moonlit room. TRACK OUT *to reveal Shannon being led by Devine. She stops.*

The dark, richly decorated suite is filled with bodies.

Devine smiles faintly, persuading her in and stumbling as he goes.

CUT BACK TO:

INT. ARTHUR'S BEDROOM – SUBURBAN MANCHESTER – NIGHT – 1973

Arthur turns the page.

FAST CUT TO:

INT. CONCERT HALL – LONDON – 1973

Curt pours over a particularly wrenching guitar solo. He half-smiles when he sees:

Brian, slinking down on his haunches, approaching. When he arrives, he drops to his knees and 'goes down' on Curt's guitar, grabbing on to his ass while he plays the instrument with his teeth.

The audience goes wild.

DISSOLVE TO:

INT. ARTHUR'S BEDROOM – NIGHT – 1973

Arthur's face, breath CLOSE, *staring at a photo of the preceding stage stunt, softly grinding.*

85

VERY CLOSE *on his open hand, circling slowly over stretching underwear.*

INT. STUART LIVING ROOM – SUBURBAN MANCHESTER – NIGHT – 1973

Mr Stuart looks up angrily from the TV toward the pounding music from Arthur's room. He glares at Mrs Stuart sitting beside him.

He throws down the newspaper and starts up the stairs.

CUT TO:

INT. HOTEL SUITE – NEW YORK – NIGHT – 1973

Two Glam Girls are leading Curt to a corner couch, bringing us to Trevor and Harley, who stand opposite each other shirtless. Angel is going down on Trevor while a Girl Groupie caresses Harley. A Boy Groupie sits beside her watching as Trevor and Harley stare at one another's bodies, stone drunk.

Mandy is lying in a throng of Skinny Boys, her tongue down Cooper's throat. A Nude Woman with large breasts pulls her away.

MANDY
Thank God – a *woman*!

Passing over a large red velvet sofa we discover a beautiful Asian Woman in bright-blue feathers undressing a man. She is accompanied by a nude Black Boy who kisses the man while pulling off his tie. The TRACK ENDS *on a* CLOSE UP *of the man. It's Brian.*

All of a sudden he glances up.

Curt stands near a window, his eyes on Brian. He has broken away from his captors.

Brian stares back, frozen. The Asian Woman tries to kiss him.

Curt just turns, disappearing down the hall.

Brian stares after.

Shannon observes the exchange, standing against a wall with Devine's head in her breasts.

CUT TO:

INT. STUART LIVING ROOM – MANCHESTER – NIGHT – 1973

Mrs Stuart stands as Mr Stuart pounds on Arthur's door – off-screen.

> MR STUART
> (*off-screen*)
> Arthur! Arthur, open this door!

We hear him forcing it open and storming in, shouting.

> (*from inside Arthur's room*)
> Could you conceivably turn down that blasted - *Jesus Christ*!

Suddenly there's a crash, followed by the screech of a phonograph needle. Mrs Stuart jolts, hurries upstairs.

We follow as she rushes down the hall to Arthur's door where she stops, looking in.

INT. ARTHUR'S BEDROOM – MANCHESTER – NIGHT – 1973

Slow ZOOM OUT from Mrs Stuart standing at the door as we hear Mr Stuart growl in low, threatening tones.

> MR STUART
> (*off-screen*)
> You bring shame to this house. You bring shame to your mother and me. It's a shameful, filthy thing you're doing –
> (*suddenly at the top of his lungs*)
> DO YOU HEAR ME?!

Mrs Stuart jumps.

> Stand up!

Mr Stuart is standing behind Arthur, who slowly stands into frame, shirtless. His nose is bleeding. ZOOM ends, revealing the dresser mirror Arthur is standing before. Pictures of his idols flank his reflection.

DISSOLVE TO:

INT. HOTEL SUITE – NEW YORK – NIGHT – 1973

VERY CLOSE *on Brian disengaging from his partners, their eyes opening, their faces looking up.* PAN UP *with Brian, standing, his eyes fixed on the hallway.*

CLOSE ON *Mandy, her eyes opening, sensing something. She spots Brian.*

Shannon continues staring as Devine's head comes up and looks over as well.

>   MANDY
>   (*voice-over*)
> It's funny how beautiful people look –

Brian, slightly SLOW MOTION, *approaching the hall. He glances back a beat before slipping into the shadows.*

> – when they're walking out the door.

FAST CUT TO:

Brief silent shots:

EXT. BUS – MANCHESTER – DAY – 1973

Arthur boards the bus to London with a single suitcase.

He sits in the back as the bus takes off.

Through the window he sees his mother running out and stopping, diminishing as we pass. Finally, she raises a hand goodbye.

>   MANDY
>   (*voice-over*)
> Now: just because someone sees, you know –

FAST RETURN TO:

INT. DIVE BAR – NEW YORK – DAY – 1984

Arthur, jolted back to the present.

>   MANDY
>   (*facetious*)
> – *two naked people* asleep in bed together . . . it doesn't
> necessarily *prove* sex was involved.

FAST CUT TO:

INT. BEDROOM SUITE – NEW YORK – DAY – 1973

Brian and Curt in bed, tangled and naked, dead asleep.

Shannon looks through a crack in the door.

> MANDY
> (*voice-over*)
> It does, however, make for a very strong case.

Shannon closes the door and Brian's eyes open.

CUT TO:

INT. HOTEL SUITE – NEW YORK – DAY – 1973

In a corner of the room Mandy consoles Shannon who is weeping.

> MANDY
> Really, luv, it shouldn't upset you so. Brian is a grown man
> and fully capable of shagging whatever he fancies and
> exceedingly partial to the practice. You know what he says,
> 'I'm a bisexual chauvinist pig!' He's quite proud of it! But
> you're a sweet, sensitive darling to be so broken up about it.
> Brian would be –

Shannon suddenly grabs Mandy's arm, glaring.

> SHANNON
> Don't you *ever* tell Brian –

> MANDY
> *Ow*! Hey –

She yanks free.

> SHANNON
> *Swear* to me you'll never breathe a word of this – *ever*!

> MANDY
> I swear. Jesus.

Mandy gets up, rubbing her wrist, and walks off, not a little spooked.

INT. HOTEL CORRIDOR – NEW YORK – DAY – 1973

Mandy stops outside Brian's door. She takes a breath before quietly turning the knob.

INT. BEDROOM SUITE – NEW YORK – AFTERNOON – 1973

CLOSE ON *Mandy peeking in.* FAST ZOOM OUT: *the room is empty. Mandy sees a note left on the pillow with her name on it. She opens it.*

> MANDY
> (*voice-over*)
> 'Sudden change in plans. Brief holiday, much needed. Back by Hammersmith. B.'

FAST CUT TO:

INT. DIVE CLUB – NEW YORK – LATE DAY – 1984

Mandy's face, thoughtful.

> MANDY
> That was it. And I knew . . . my time with Brian, for all practical purposes, was up.

*[Two more drinks are set down by the Bartender.

> I mean, we were still married – Thanks, Ricky – But it was exceedingly clear I had no more part in his life.

She lifts her glass.

> Cheers.

> ARTHUR
> Cheers.

They drink, as the sound of waves emerge in the distance.]

> MANDY
> I'm sorry. I wish I could help you more. You seem like a nice guy. I just –

The Bartender glances up. FAST ZOOM/RACK OUT *to Mandy in foreground.*

*Cut from completed film.

90

– don't think I have what you're looking for.

Arthur smiles, looking down.

                    ARTHUR
See . . . I think you do actually.

                    MANDY
                 (*a sly smile*)
Oh yeah? And what makes you think so?

                    ARTHUR
That smile, for one thing.

Her smiles stays.

                    MANDY
Well. Smiles lie.

                    ARTHUR
Exactly.

Mandy sighs. A faint melody rises with the waves.

                    MANDY
Listen, once – of course – there was a gorgeous gorgeous
time. And we were living our dreams, indifferent to all life
that was not social life. But you see all that went away – all of
it –
                  (*quietly*)
– with Curt.

Music builds to 'My Unclean'/Wylde Rattz as slow ZOOMS *begin on
each of them.*

And not even the real Curt. It was the idea of Curt more than
anything, this – image. That no one, of course, could ever
possibly live up to. I mean Maxwell Demon, Curt Wild – they
were *fictions*! And somewhere along the way, Brian just
seemed to get lost in the lie.

DISSOLVE TO:

INT. RECORDING STUDIO – LONDON – NIGHT – 1974

TRACK *past hands adjusting levels on a sixteen-track mixer, and on past the faces of visitors seated in the back: Trevor and Girlfriend, Devine and Mandy.*

> MANDY
> (*voice-over*)
> But when it all came crashing down, I watched from the sidelines just like everybody else.

TRACK OUT *from Curt at the mike in the soundproof booth. He starts to sing, eyes closed.*

In the foreground, Brian is revealed watching through the glass, his back to camera. When Curt doesn't come in on the next verse, Brian twitches angrily.

> BRIAN
> *Shit!*

> DEVINE
> Cut it.

> MIXER
> Should I stop it?

Brian turns around, facing Devine and the Mixer who sits behind him at the board.

Curt continues singing.

Brian watches, biting his thumb.

He's gonna hit the bridge a half-verse early.

> DEVINE
>
> Now you're simply wasting tape.

> BRIAN
>
> Alright. Cut it.

The music stops.

Behind Brian, Curt looks up. He starts hollering through the glass but we can't hear him. Brian is frozen, his back to the booth. The Mixer switches Curt on.

> CURT
> (*on intercom*)
>
> Answer me.

Brian turns around to face him.

Curt glares at him through the glass, awaiting an answer.

INSIDE BOOTH

From Curt's POV we see Brian. We see him say 'What?'

> CURT
>
> *Why'd* you cut? *Why*?!

Brian's quiet response is monitored for Curt but barely heard. Through the glass we can read his lips.

> BRIAN
> (*on intercom*)
>
> Because you missed your cue.
> (*looks down, quieter*)
>
> Again.

CURT

What? *What?*

CONTROL ROOM

Devine leans into the intercom and chimes in, tersely.

Brian leans in.

DEVINE

We're sorry, Curt, but it appears as if you –

BRIAN
(*smoothly*)

Curt, we only ask that *when* you decide to make a change you simply inform us in advance so Eton is properly prepared, *otherwise* –

Curt turns violently, thrusting his arm as he curses.

CURT
(*on intercom*)

What the fuck are you talking about? – I didn't *make* any fucking change! Brian, what're you –
(*jerking away in frustration*)
Fucking mother-fucker!

DEVINE

Eton – please.

The Mixer switches Curt off. We watch him continue to rave in silence as Brian listens to Devine.

Brian, I'm sorry to be the one to say it, but what began as an interesting experiment has quite frankly descended into a demeaning waste of your time and mine. You've already spent – what? – forty hours studio time –

BRIAN

Thirty-six.

DEVINE

Whatever! Thirty-six hours – on two, three bloody cuts! You don't seem to realize it, Brian, but you're a very big star now

94

and your time is worth a great deal more than this –

Brian himself switches on the intercom and Curt's shrieks come searing on.

> CURT
> – fucking queen bitch space-god on some fucking high horse! You and your fucking henchmen! –

Brian switches it off and responds quickly and quietly.

> BRIAN
> Perhaps it's time for another little break. What do you say, fellas?
>> (*a wan smile*)
>
> Give us a stretch?
>> (*and to Devine*)
>
> Jerry?

Devine stands, coolly.

> DEVINE
> I can't risk extending his contract, Brian. I think it's quite clear why. I'll speak to you tomorrow.

He turns and begins filing out with the others. RACK *to Brian in the foreground, watching Curt.*

He has begun throwing chairs around the booth. Brian turns away, black in shadow. Everyone has gone but Mandy, who watches Brian from a dark corner.

For a split second his sadness shows. Then his eyes flash up and he sees her.

She looks him in the eye. Then she turns and leaves the room. We follow. As the door shuts behind her, and the sound of Curt's shouts resume in the distance, a tender instrumental of the previous song rises.

Mandy passes through shadows, into moonlight.

EXT. RECORDING STUDIO – NIGHT – 1974

Mandy looks up.

The sky is full of stars. Then – suddenly – there's a crash of doors.

In a massive LONG SHOT *Mandy watches Curt come tearing out of a rear door. The third-story window bangs open and Brian's head sticks out, shouting after him. There is blood on his mouth.*

> BRIAN
>
> Piss off, then! Go on!

Yards away, the technicians stare blankly at the spectacle.

> Back to your wolves! Your junkie twerps! Your bloody shock treatment! And fuck you too!

Mandy watches

Brian watching

Curt vanish.

We hear Brian's voice singing 'Bittersweet'/Roxy Music.

CUT TO:

INT. BRIAN'S OFFICE – DAY – 1974

Curtain parts, revealing Curt below on the street.

He looks up and sees Brian.

EXT. BIJOU OFFICE – DAY – 1974

Brian looks through the window then withdraws. Curt gets into the limo and takes off.

INT. BRIAN'S OFFICE – DAY – 1974

A phone receiver is lifted up. CLOSE ON *Brian's finger dialing a number.*

INT. LIMO – MOMENTS LATER – DAY – 1974

The streets of London passing from a car.

Curt looks out. He squints from the sun.

Signs for Heathrow Airport approach.

    CUT TO:

INT. BRIAN'S OFFICE – DAY – LATER – 1974

CLOSE ON *Brian's tight mouth against a phone receiver.*

BRIAN

    Out. O-U-T.

    CUT TO:

INT. BIJOU OFFICES – DEVINE'S OFFICE – DAY – 1974

CLOSE ON *Devine's nose, the phone against his face. Speedy* ZOOM OUT.

DEVINE

Well, Brian, I'm afraid that's rather out of the question. You are contractually bound to complete the Maxwell Demon tour *as* Maxwell Demon –

Mandy stands at the door of his office holding a stack of papers. CLOSE ON *Devine.*

BRIAN

(*off-screen; faintly through receiver*)

Jerry, I'm telling you, the whole thing is just getting far too out of hand – I really don't think I'll be able to –

DEVINE

(*looking at Mandy*)

Brian – Brian – I realize you're under tremendous strain, but you've just gotta hang on in there and finish . . .

Mandy slowly turns to go.

– the bloody tour. You hang on in there. I'll hang on here.

CUT TO:

INT. BRIAN'S OFFICE – DAY

Brian is in total distress. He is not paying attention to what Devine is saying.

DEVINE

And then you can do what you want, OK?

CUT TO:

EXT. STREETS OF KREUZBERG – BERLIN – NIGHT – 1974

Curt walks through an industrial neighborhood in West Berlin. He lights a cigarette as an elevated train passes in the distance, blinking red and green. Suddenly he looks up, spotting something on the street.

An individual looking remarkably like Brian, dressed as Maxwell Demon, stands with two other flashly dressed individuals.

Curt squints at the spectre, taking a few vague steps in his direction.

The figure turns, revealing himself to be a teenage fan.

Curt, CLOSE, spooked by the misrecognition.

CUT TO:

EXT. PICCADILLY CIRCUS – NIGHT – 1973

Arthur walks through seedy, sparkly Piccadilly carrying his suitcase.

Shots of the people: men in trenchcoats, teenagers sitting on the stairs of Piccadilly fountain, Japanese tourists.

Arthur sees a group of Glam Girls stumble into a dark club. He follows.

CUT TO:

INT. LAST RESORT CLUB – NIGHT – 1973

In a cramped London club, Malcolm, Ray, Pearl and Billy of The Flaming Creatures (a cross between Roxy Music and The New York Dolls) perform the current section of 'Bittersweet' with raucous intensity.

Arthur watches. He likes what he hears.

Ray spots him and blows him a trampy kiss.

Arthur blushes.

CUT TO:

EXT. BRIAN SLADE PROTESTS – LONDON – DAY – 1974 VIDEO NEWSREELS

CLOSE ON *grainy shot of a Brian Slade poster in flames over the song's tender finish.*

We see albums being burned and thrown into a charred pile. Others burn songbooks, magazines, forty-fives.

INT. BIJOU OFFICES – DAY – 1974

Brian's face, staring at the monitor, a ghost of his former self.

CLOSE ON *his hand rewinding the tape.*

CUT TO:

INT. LAST RESORT CLUB – LATER – 1973

TRACK *through the slowed-down remains of the club, most of the clientele subdued with drink. Off-screen, The Flaming Creatures' late-night banter is heard:*

MALCOLM

I don't believe there is much of a future to speak of –

PEARL

We're in a bit of a decadence spiral, aren't we?

We pass one half-undressed Weimar Woman, evoking thirties Berlin,
spread across the tables.

BILLY

Sinking fast.

RAY

Big Brother, baby. All the way.

Reveal Arthur and the Creatures, sprawled around a table teaming with
empty pints.

Quick SINGLES *on each of them:*

MALCOLM

Which is why we prefer impressions to ideas –

PEARL

Brief flights to sustained ones –

RAY

Exceptions to types –

BILLY

Situations to subjects –

PEARL

And yourself?

Arthur looks at them a moment.

ARTHUR

Well I'm - really just looking for a room at the moment.

DISSOLVE TO:

EXT. KREUZBERG – BERLIN – NIGHT – 1974

Curt has inadvertently joined a hustler/cruising strip, full of young
specimens on street corners and pulled-over cars. As Curt walks he
notices one car beginning to follow.

He smiles to himself, thinking it's a proposition, and turns the next corner.

The car does the same.

Up ahead the light changes, and Curt makes a run for the intersection.

The car speeds up after him but stops at the red light.

As Curt crosses the street, passing the front of the car, he slows, trying to get a look at the driver.

Suddenly he stops, spooked.

CLOSE ON *a car window rolling down and revealing Jack Fairy, who lifts pink glasses and smiles.*

Curt blinks, and approaches the car in a bit of a fog.

The car door opens, and Jack Fairy extends his hand.

CUT TO:

INT. RECORDING STUDIO – LATER THAT NIGHT – 1974

Brian records his version of the song alone in the darkened studio. He returns to its tender refrain with eyes closed, heart clenched.

In the hallway Mandy moves through shadows toward the studio, drawn by the music.

Inside a CLOSE TRACK *curls around Brian, revealing a perfect tear glittering on his cheek.*

Mandy is stunned by his tenderness.

CUT TO:

INT. DIVE CLUB – NEW YORK – LATE DAY – 1984

CLOSE ON *Mandy.*

> MANDY
> So for one entire day I actually think Brian's been shot, that the whole thing is real, all his paranoias proven horribly true –

ARTHUR

You mean – no one told you –

MANDY

Nope.

ARTHUR

Why?

MANDY

Forgot.

ARTHUR

Jesus.

MANDY

I mean . . . I knew it was over. I just didn't know it was up to
me to make it stop.

CUT TO:

INT. BIJOU TOWNHOUSE ENTRANCE – DAY – 1975

We follow Mandy up the unlit stairway leading to the old offices.

*At the top of the stairs the door is slightly ajar. Mandy pushes it open
and enters.*

INT. BIJOU OFFICES – DAY 1975

*Inside, the office's musical comedy ambience has turned film noir:
shadows engulf the cavernous space where desks are piled with boxes,
and chairs stacked or overturned.*

*She walks through the deserted cubicles, passing shady remnants of the
past.*

*Against a far wall, the TV monitor is playing more silent footage from
the Slade protests.*

*There is a sudden bang and Mandy jolts, turning to the French doors
hitting the wall with the wind. White curtains blow into the room.*

Mandy looks down.

There, in the far corner of the room on a large mattress sits Brian.

Shirtless, he is snorting lines of cocaine off the ass of a nude black girl (Coco), who is dead asleep. On a lone coffee table – the only other furniture in sight – a mountain of cocaine has spilled over paraphernalia and hundred-dollar bills.

> BRIAN
> (*weak*)

Mandy.

> MANDY

Hello, Brian.

Brian just stares for a few dumbfounded seconds before offering her the straw.

> MANDY
> (*barely maintaining*)

No thanks.

Mandy stares at him, almost smiling, before she turns to get something out of her bag. Slow TRACK IN *begins as she shuffles through her belongings. She produces a folder and holds it out to him.*

MATCH TRACK IN *on Brian, who stares at the folder, then back up at Mandy.*

She remains frozen, arm outstretched.

These are the papers. I believe they're in order. All you need to do is sign.

Brian watches as she turns and walks across the room to the coffee table.

Mandy sticks the folder into the pile of coke.

So you won't forget.

Brian blinks in confusion.

She sticks a ballpoint pen in as well and looks back at him. Brian stares, his face suddenly open like a child's.

> BRIAN

I already have.

Coco squirms in her sleep, tightening her grip around Brian.

MANDY

Evidently.

With that, Mandy turns and starts out the door. Then all at once she stops and turns to face him.

Fuck you, Brian. Did you *ever* – for one bloody second in your life want anything *more* –
>> (*suddenly quiet*)
– than *this*?

Brief pause.

BRIAN
(*suddenly lucid*)

No.

Mandy looks at him, her eyes filling, with a sad smile.

MANDY
(*softly*)

Your problem is: 'You get what you want and do what you will.'

BRIAN
(*matching her in a sudden game of quotation*)
'Worlds,' Mandy, 'are built out of suffering. There is suffering at the birth of a child as at the birth of a star.'

MANDY

'You live in terror of not being misunderstood.'

BRIAN

'Women defend themselves by attacking, just as they attack by suddcn and strange surrenders.'

CLOSE ON *Mandy, her eyes moist.*

MANDY
(*more to herself*)
'I lost my girlhood, true. But it was for you.'

Suddenly a rear door bangs open, startling Mandy and waking Coco.

Shannon stands at the doorway, staring at Mandy. Now Brian's personal secretary, Shannon's force has grown considerably. Coco opens her eyes and lifts her head.

> SHANNON
> (*professionally irate*)
> What in God's name is going on here? How on earth did you get up here?! Brian, I'm really sorry about that.

> BRIAN
> That's alright, Shannon. Mandy was just leaving.

> SHANNON
> Mandy, if you would please be so kind as to follow me –

Shannon takes Mandy firmly in hand and Mandy recoils, furiously.

> MANDY
> Let go of me. I'm perfectly capable of making my own –

> SHANNON
> I really don't want to have to call someone –

> MANDY
> *Call* someone? Who the hell do you think you are? I'm his wife, for fuck's sake!

Brian and Coco start giggling.

Mandy's eyes fill with tears. Enraged, she turns and sweeps the pile of cocaine into the air.

> Fuck the lot of you!

Briefly SLOW MOTION: Brian, laughing through the white cloud, divorce papers flying.

> CUT TO:

EXT. CHELSEA STREET – LATE AFTERNOON – 1975

High aerial view of Mandy streaming from the building and across the street, her long shadow stretching the length of the road.

Quiet music holds under.

MANDY
(*voice-over*)
And I ran like hell and didn't look back.

CUT TO:

INT. DIVE CLUB – NEW YORK – LATE DAY – 1984

CLOSE ON *the back of Mandy's head, looking out on to hazy New York.*

ARTHUR
(*off-screen*)
Was that the last time you saw him?

Mandy turns to look at him.

Arthur sits at the table, a few yards away.

MANDY
No. But it *was* the last time we – actually spoke.

A distant trace of music begins as Arthur looks up from his notes. A slow TRACK IN *begins.*

Mandy stands, passing Arthur on her way to the bar.

I saw him again – briefly – a few weeks later. At a concert.

ARTHUR
He was – performing?

TRACK IN *behind Mandy at the cigarette machine.*

MANDY
No. Curt was actually performing. He and Jack Fairy had just finished their Berlin record and Curt was in London playing some gigs. And Brian was there – for a second. I don't think anyone even saw him.

Music and TRACK *converge as Mandy pushes the button. Her cigarettes drop.*

CLOSE ON *Arthur.*

ARTHUR

What – *which* concert?

Mandy turns to him.

SUDDEN CUT TO:

INT. RAINBOW THEATRE – LONDON – NIGHT – 1975

An ominous crash of Organ announces the majesty of the old hall: red velvet curtains curling up beneath its opulent proscenium, framing the stage like a golden crown.

Cheers and Music spill into:

INT. CREATURES' FLAT – NIGHT – 1975

Teenage Arthur, CLOSE *in the mirror, is making himself up as Maxwell Demon.*

The table is strewn with a mess of make-up and magic mushrooms.

Arthur pauses to regard his feminine self as the sound of applause turns to unrest.

We hear:

*[MALE VOICE
                  (*an amplified whisper*)
  Maxwell Demon! Star of my eyes!

Violent booing and shouting.

RETURN TO:

INT. RAINBOW THEATRE – NIGHT – 1975

The face of Brian Slade as Maxwell Demon is projected across a scrim on-stage and much of the audience howls in revolt.

Arthur stands with the Creatures in the audience. The crowd around him is not exactly taken with his costume. One guy shoves him and Ray and Billy immediately intercept.

---

*Cut from completed film.

108

MALE VOICE
(*resuming over the outburst*)
Curt Wild, Polly Small, Roxy, Dolls and Fairys all.

With each name more faces are projected, and the shouts give way to cheers.

On-stage, through the final projections, the silhouette of a looming coffin is revealed against deep purple lights, with its lid slowly opening. A beam of golden light rises from the coffin, illuminating a slow cascade of glitter.]

The scrim is lifted just as a caped figure emerges, walking into opal light. It's Jack Fairy, looking as tall and radiant as ever.

Jack resumes his narration over rousing applause.

JACK
To save your wild, wild lives
To ne'er your fans embitter

SWOOPING IN *on Arthur, his face amid the sea of spectators. There's a panic in his eyes.*

To cease your sad demise tonight
We toast –

FAST CUT TO:

INT. DIVE CLUB – NEW YORK – LATE DAY – 1984

Mandy, CLOSE.

MANDY
It was like a tribute – a sort of farewell concert to glam rock. I think they even called it –

FAST RETURN:

INT. RAINBOW THEATRE – ON-STAGE – NIGHT – 1975

Music peaks as an enormous banner unfurls like a flame. Its gilded script reads: THE DEATH OF GLITTER SHOW!

A rockin' Flaming Creatures song ('20th Century Boy'/T-Rex) begins.

INT. WINGS – RAINBOW THEATRE – LATER – 1975

Fast ZOOM OUT *from Arthur, dancing wildly in the wings.*

INT. RAINBOW THEATRE – ON-STAGE – NIGHT – 1975

The Creatures perform to a spirited audience.

In the wings a Roadie puts his hand on Arthur's shoulder to settle him down.

Arthur turns, embarrassed. He catches sight of:

Three people approaching from backstage: a Musician, a Hip Woman with a clipboard – and Curt Wild. ZOOM IN.

Arthur stares in disbelief.

We hear:

> ADULT ARTHUR
> (*voice-over*)
> I'm trying to reach Curt Wild. I'm a journalist from the *Herald.*

Swirling music over

CUT TO:

EXT. NEW YORK ALLEY – TELEPHONE BOOTH – DAY – 1984

TRACK *around Arthur in a payphone.*

> ARTHUR
> Yes – hello this is Arthur Stuart from the *Herald.* I've been trying to reach Curt Wild for a story I'm doing. I was told I might be able to reach him at this number – Hello? Hello?

INT. OFFICE – NEW YORK – LATE DAY – 1984

MATCH TRACK *around the back of Curt's head, on the phone to Arthur. He sits at the desk of a small, ratty office.*

CURT

Listen, man, I don't know who the hell gave you this number
– but Curt Wild is not available and not interested in granting
you or anyone else an interview on this subject – you get it?

ARTHUR

I'm sorry – I was told –

*Curt slams down the phone. He looks over to two suits with
Government insignias sitting opposite on a tattered couch.*

RETURN TO:

EXT. NEW YORK STREET - LATE DAY – 1984

*Arthur hangs up the phone. He shakes his head as cheerless music begins
'Gimme Danger'/Iggy and the Stooges. He turns and sets off down the
street as we* BOOM UP.

Music builds as we follow Arthur in CLOSE-UP, *fighting back
memories. Finally, he shuts his eyes.*

DISSOLVE TO:

INT. RAINBOW THEATRE – ON-STAGE – NIGHT – 1975

Dark, golden glimpses of a sinewy body, moving to the music.

*Curt performs his last song to Brian, a mournful plea for submission. He
is dressed in thigh-high go-go boots and red panties and throughout the
song he cowers and crawls.*

CLOSE TRACK *in to Arthur, watching from the wings, surrounded by
The Creatures.*

Curt sings with tender, ominous restraint, letting loose only at the end.

In the wings Arthur turns and sees:

Mandy, slowly walking toward the stage.

On-stage Curt sings with seething intensity.

*When the song finally erupts into a swarm of guitars, Curt breaks into
desperate thrashes across the stage.*

In the wings Arthur sneaks another glance at:

Mandy, watching Curt with a furrowed brow. Suddenly she turns and looks out to the rear of the auditorium.

Arthur follows her gaze.

From the back of the house a figure steps into view, silhouetted against the light of an exit door.

Arthur squints to make it out.

CLOSER, *we see that it's Brian.*

On-stage Curt's thrashing continues. He has cut himself and blood can be seen on his neck and chest. It reaches a peak as the deep blue lights slowly fade to black. There is a split second of silence before the crowd explodes.

CLOSE ON *Brian, who slips away.*

CUT TO:

INT. RAINBOW THEATRE – BACKSTAGE – MOMENTS LATER – 1975

In relative darkness, the Roadie is clearing a path for the band to exit the stage, cornering Arthur. Dark, wet bodies crash past.

As Curt comes darting by, Mandy suddenly bolts past the Roadie and grabs him.

CLOSE ON *Arthur, cornered by their hug. He hears:*

> MANDY
>
> Really.

> CURT
>
> Thanks.

Houselights come up and Mandy and Curt disengage, speaking quietly to one another.

Arthur looks down, trying to listen inconspicuously.

> (*quietly*)
>
> Did you . . . ?

MANDY
(*also quietly*)
I didn't see him.

Then she turns, catching sight of Arthur.

Curt looks up as well.

Arthur stands caught, a doe-eyed Maxwell Demon.

For a moment, Curt is taken aback by Arthur's youthful homage.

'Dead Finks Don't Talk'/Brian Eno begins.

CUT TO:

INT. ARTHUR'S APARTMENT – NEW YORK – LATE AFTERNOON –
1984

CLOSE-UP *Arthur, standing and looking in the mirror of his apartment.
For a few beats he is still. Then, suddenly, we hear the clatter of
electronics. Arthur turns.*

ZOOM IN *to his desk where he is receiving a telex.*

HIGH ANGLE: *Arthur walks across the room to his desk. His apartment
is a crooked, looming container, twice as tall as it is wide. Its few
bunker-style windows are strangely high.*

EXTREME CLOSE-UP: *telex.*

It reads:
'NAME CHANGE SEARCH: BRIAN SLADE – REQUEST DENIED'

ARTHUR
Shit

Arthur pulls out the chair to his desk.

CUT TO:

LATER

Computer screen. Words flash by:

'FILE REQUEST FOR NAME CHANGE SEARCH:

114

Arthur's face as he searches, blue in the glow of his computer. The TV blares in the background.

TV NEWS
(*off-screen*)
Sponsored by President Reynolds' Redeem America Committee, the campaign fundraiser headlined pop superstar Tommy Stone, and raised over a million dollars for the Committee to Prosper. Also performing on the bill, Pat Boone, the Chuck Damon Singers and Martha Gale.

On computer screen: Brian Slade's real name and birthplace appear:

BRIAN SLADE, *born: Thomas Brian Stoningham Slade, 2 January 1949, in Birmingham, Great Britain.*

Name change: 16 March 1971 [Brian Slade], 23 October 1979 [WITHHELD]

We hear:

Meanwhile, talk of another airlift for the South Florida famine is being discussed in Los Angeles. While in business news today, the Ticketron corporation announced unprecedented record sales for the Tommy Stone World Tour, which kicks off here in New York later this month.

Arthur glances up from his computer.

TV SCREEN

Shannon, brittle for her age, speaks into a mike. Beside her sits Tommy Stone.

SHANNON
(*on TV*)
. . . Due to the overwhelming demand, additional shows are being added whenever and wherever possible.

TRACK IN *to Arthur who is stuck, watching.*

> TV NEWS
> (*off-screen*)
> According to a spokesman for the tour, the six additional
> Anaheim shows sold out in a record fifteen minutes.

Suddenly he races back to his computer.

On computer screen, CLOSE UP *across Brian Slade's birth-name:*
THOMAS BRIAN PATRICK STONINGHAM SLADE.

TRACK INTO *the names* 'THOMAS . . . STONINGHAM'

Arthur stares at the screen.

He looks back at the TV set. FAST PAN/ZOOM INTO *TV screen.*

> SHANNON
> (*on TV*)
> Regrettably, Mr Stone only has time for a few brief questions
> this morning as he is scheduled to catch a plane to Zurich –

> REPORTERS
> (*on TV*)
> Tommy! Tommy! Tommy!

TRACK INTO *screen, as music flares. Tommy Stone bears a marked
resemblance to Brian Slade.*

CUT TO:

EXT. NEW YORK STREETS – SUNSET – 1984

*Music continues as Arthur runs through the rush hour crowds of New
York.*

⋆[EXT. NEWS OFFICE – NEW YORK – LATE DAY – 1984

*Arthur runs up the steps of the building, passing everyone leaving for the
day.*

> MURRAY
> What's chasin' you, my son?

⋆Cut from completed film.

116

                    ARTHUR
Is Lou still here?

                    MURRAY
Might be. He had a late appointment – There, that one.

*He gestures to a well-dressed woman marching out of the building.
Arthur recognizes her as Shannon.*

                    ARTHUR
Thanks, Murray.

Arthur runs into the building.]

INT. NEWSROOM CORRIDOR – NIGHT – 1984

Arthur races down the shadowy hallway to Lou's office. He knocks.

                    ARTHUR
Lou? Lou?

*He opens the door. It's dark inside. He hears a sound and looks back to
the elevators.*

The doors are opening and Lou is getting in.

Lou!

Arthur goes running down the hall.

Lou! *LOU!*

                    LOU
I'm sorry, Arthur. I'm late.

                    ARTHUR
Lou – please! I think I just stumbled on to something.
Something quite big.

Lou presses a button and the doors open.

                    LOU
What?

                    ARTHUR
I think I know who Brian Slade is.

                    LOU
    The story's been dropped.

                    ARTHUR
    What? *Why?*

The elevator doors are closing.

                    LOU
    I need you on the Stone show.

                    ARTHUR
    But that's –

                    LOU
    I'm sorry, Arthur.

The doors close.

                    ARTHUR
    What did she say to you? *Lou!*

A slow build of music begins.

    DISSOLVE TO:

EXT. NEW YORK STREETS – NIGHT – 1984

Arthur stares at a poster of Tommy Stone on a bus stop.

CLOSE ON *Arthur, staring sadly. Music continues rising as we hear:*

                    ARTHUR
                    (*voice-over*)
    It's only now, looking back, that I see –

    DISSOLVE TO:

INT. RAINBOW THEATRE – LOBBY – NIGHT – 1975

SLOW MOTION TRACK *in to Curt, surrounded by colorful figures and
painted faces at a packed, post-show reception. Everyone is laughing,
drinking and grabbing one another, but the colors have faded, the glitter
worn, and a dark, Berlin-style decadence has set in.* TRACK *ends as
Curt looks up, spotting someone from across the room.*

MATCH TRACK *in to Arthur, squeezed into the corner of the lobby, trapped by Curt's glance.*

> ARTHUR
> (*voice-over*)
>
> – how you patched through my walls and entered my life . . . in waves.

Arthur looks down shyly and back up again.

Curt's eyes are fixed.

FAST DISSOLVE TO:

EXT. RAINBOW THEATRE ROOF – 4 A.M. – 1975

CLOSE BACK-TRACK *with Arthur as he walks across the dark rooftop. Shadows pass over his face like ghosts.*

The music yields to Curt's deep, internal whisper:

> CURT
> (*voice-over; slow, thoughtful*)
>
> Come closer. Don't be frightened. What's your name? Your favourite color? Song. Movie. Don't be nervous. Are you high?

Arthur whispers his response aloud, half to himself:

> ARTHUR
>
> I'm on a button.

FAST DISSOLVE TO:

EXT. RAINBOW THEATRE – ROOFTOP – LATER – 1975

Curt busts up laughing, opening a can of beer that sprays all over himself. He sits with Arthur at the far corner of the roof, shirtless.

CLOSE ON *Arthur's face, speckled with beer. Curt looks up.*

> CURT
>
> Hey –

Arthur follows, just catching sight of:

A falling star.

                              (*off-screen*)
Make a wish.

FAST DISSOLVE TO EARLIER:

EXT. RAINBOW THEATRE – ROOF – EARLIER – 1975

Wide TRACK IN *on Curt, who sits at the far end of the roof watching our approach (Arthur's POV during his previous walk).*

A voice returns but it's Adult Arthur we hear.

                          ADULT ARTHUR
                           (*voice-over*)
He was waiting for me. I had followed his signals and slipped away and now – suddenly –

CUT TO:

EXT. RAINBOW THEATRE – ROOF – LATER – 1975

Music continues as we follow Curt's hand as it travels to Arthur and lands tenderly on his cheek.

Arthur is pulling off his shirt, standing over Curt who is also shirtless.

FAST DISSOLVE:

EXT. RAINBOW THEATRE – ROOF – LATER – 1975

EXTREME CLOSE-UP *of Curt's hand on Arthur's bare back, his cool white skin filling the screen. We follow it down.*

FAST CUT TO:

EXT. RAINBOW THEATRE – ROOF – MORNING – 1975

Curt laughs hysterically.

FAST RETURN TO:

EXT. RAINBOW THEATRE – ROOF – NIGHT – 1975

In sweaty CLOSE-UP, *Curt sees something in the sky.*

> CURT
> Hey –

Arthur's eye darts up. He sees:

A luminous spacecraft, like the one that passed over Old Dublin. It swirls over London with a thunderous boom –

– and vanishes.

All that remains is a sky full of glitterdust.

CLOSE ON *Curt's lips, whispering through the cascade:*

> Make a wish –

A WIDE SHOT *of the roof, now awash in stardust, as the white bodies of Curt and Arthur are seen through the sparkles; Curt behind Arthur, gently fucking. A long, slow* CRANE OUT *begins, as music and voices peak.*

> And see yourself, on-stage, inside-out! A tangle of garlands in your hair. Of course you are pleasantly surprised.

> TEEN ARTHUR
> (*voice-over*)
> Softly, he said . . .

> ALL THREE VOICES
> (*whispering*)
> I will mangle your mind.

We withdraw as the bodies of Curt and Arthur are engulfed and the artificiality of the set intensifies, warping perspective in the style of Caligari.

INT. STAGE – GRAND BALLROOM SET – NIGHT

The TRACK *continues, revealing the bombed-out remains of a grand ballroom, and Brian, turning to camera, dressed as a bejeweled Maxwell Demon. He brings a microphone to his lips and begins to sing, ('Tumbling Down'/Steve Harley Cockney Rebel), slowly descending a gnarled staircase as we* PULL OUT.

He stops at a half-blown landing just as a tattered chandelier is raised into frame. He mounts the shimmering beast, and finds a wreath of flowers around its cable. As he ascends, he throws flowers out to the audience below.

With a flower between his teeth he reaches out to the audience just as the lights flicker into darkness. Maxwell Demon is gone.

Cheers.

INT. STADIUM SHOW – NEW YORK – NIGHT – 1984

Arthur sits in the audience, applauding, coming out of his reverie.

Briefly:

INT. STADIUM SHOW – ON-STAGE – NIGHT – 1984

We see the actual show: Tommy Stone in glitzy white garb, arms open, receiving applause and bouquets of flowers.

> CUT TO:

EXT. MADISON SQUARE GARDEN – NIGHT – 1984

Arthur walks out of the theatre to 'Dead Finks Don't Talk'/Brian Eno. Fans are rushing past. Up ahead, a small crowd has gathered around the stage door.

There are cheers as Tommy Stone appears.

A huge spotlight is turned on to the door.

Arthur stops and watches.

> REPORTERS
> Tommy! Tommy! Where did you get the idea for such a brilliant theatrical stadium show?

> TOMMY
> Tell you the truth – it's a bloody pain in the ass! The whole thing takes six full-size rigs or three chartered planes to transport. What can I say? I think big!

Arthur approaches the crowd.

Tommy! What's your opinion of the work President Reynolds
has been doing –

TOMMY

Excellent. Excellent. I think he's doing brilliant work. He's a
– tremendous leader, tremendous spokesperson for the needs
of the nation today –

Suddenly Arthur yells out over the others:

ARTHUR

Tommy! What is your response to the recent allegations
connecting you to bisexual pop singer Brian Slade, who
staged his own assassination ten years ago this week in
London?

Tommy is white.

Briefly:

*[SILENT IMAGE

SLOW MOTION: *Brian Slade being shot on-stage.*

BACK TO:]

EXT. MADISON SQUARE GARDEN – NEW YORK – NIGHT – 1984

Reporters swarm as Arthur watches

Tommy, devoured by Security Men, whisked away.

Shannon is suddenly at the mike.

SHANNON

I'm sorry, ladies and gentlemen, that's all the questions Mr
Stone has time for this evening. Thank you very much –

Arthur, still behind the chaos of Reporters.

CUT TO:

---

*Cut from completed film.

INT. TOMMY'S DRESSING ROOM – NEW YORK – NIGHT – 1984

Music as we follow Shannon and various Assistants escorting Tommy back to his dressing room.

In the background TV news is heard:

> ### TV
> Tonight, the Tri-State Area pulls out all the stops in welcoming pop superstar Tommy Stone to Madison Square Garden. Stone is promoting his Grammy-winning release, 'People Rockin' People', to sold-out arenas worldwide . . .

Tommy is silent in the midst of a cool panic.

> ### SHANNON
> *Out! Now!* Shut the door!

CLOSE ON *Shannon, eyes shut, as people clear. When the door closes, we hear a squeal like Little Richard's coming from the TV.*

Tommy looks over.

TV SCREEN

The news broadcast of the Tommy Stone concert cuts to a clip. Suddenly Tommy Stone in white tuxedo turns to camera: a green-faced Maxwell Demon smiles eerily at Tommy Stone, taunting him through the airwaves.

MATCH TRACK *into Tommy, looking precisely as if he's seen a ghost.*

Rising music suddenly ends.

> CUT TO:

INT. MIDTOWN BAR – NEW YORK – NIGHT – 1984

The door shuts behind Arthur in a dark mid-town bar.

Everyone looks up. There is a strange between-songs silence.

Arthur proceeds, self-consciously.

A Tommy Stone song begins on the jukebox. ('People Rockin' People'/ Shudder to Think) but people in the bar continue staring at Arthur.

He approaches the bar.

ARTHUR

Beer, please.

Arthur notices a group of mostly black Teenagers, decked out in Tommy Stone gear. They whisper to each other. One Teenage Girl starts walking over.

The Bartender hands Arthur his beer, staring all the while at Arthur's jacket.

Arthur realizes he's still wearing his press pass and starts taking it off.

TEENAGE GIRL

Excuse me, sir. Are you from the Tommy Stone Tour?

ARTHUR

No. Just a journalist. Perhaps you'd like my press pass as a souvenir?

Her eyes widen. Arthur hands her the badge.

TEENAGE GIRL

Thank you, sir.

She runs back to show her friends as Arthur turns and walks deeper into the long, narrow bar.

He passes the jukebox, and discovers a second bar in the back: smaller and moodier. A man in a leather jacket is drinking alone.

Arthur stops. He can't believe his eyes.

It's Curt Wild, folding a Tommy Stone guest pass into origami.

Arthur smiles and starts advancing before even deciding to.

Curt looks up.

ARTHUR

Hi.

Curt just glares.

ARTHUR

You're Curt Wild, right?

(*irritable*)
Yeah? Who the hell are you?

Brief silence.

ARTHUR
I'm a journalist. With the *Herald*. You were at the concert?

Curt just stares at him.

It's just funny because . . . well, I was just trying to contact
you actually. For a story I was doing –

Curt takes a long swig of beer.

– about an old friend of yours? Brian Slade?

Curt looks up for a moment, hiding his interest.

Was trying to find out . . . what actually happened to him.

CURT
Look –

ARTHUR
I mean, before he became –

Curt stops.

Tight on Arthur, peeking up at him.

    – such a mystery.

Curt snorts out a sudden guffaw.

> CURT
>
> Look, man, I don't know who you've been talking to or what you're after here, but . . .
>
>   *(trails off)*

> ARTHUR
>
> What?

Curt just looks at him.

    What?

> CURT
>
> Listen – a real artist creates beautiful things and . . . puts nothing of his own life into them. Okay?

> ARTHUR
>
> Is that what you did?

CURT

No.
>   (*brief silence*)
No. We set out to change the world and ended up . . . just
changing ourselves.

ARTHUR

What's wrong with that?

CURT

Nothing!
>   (*silence*)
If you don't look at the world.

Quiet music under slow PAN *past kids gathered at the jukebox, cliques of
Tommy Stone fans, conservative, bored. One gay Latino Boy sits
braiding a girl's hair. End on a huge Tommy Stone poster.*

>   (*off-screen*)
I guess in the end he got what he wanted.

*Curt stands in thought another beat before slipping on his jacket and
downing his beer.*

CLOSE ON *Arthur looking up at him with a distant smile.*

ARTHUR

That's quite a – pin you got there.

CLOSE ON *Curt's jacket: the antique emerald pin sparkles green.*

CURT

Oh yeah.

ARTHUR

Is it old?

CURT
>   (*examining it*)
Possibly. It was Oscar Wilde's. Or so I was told by the person
who gave it to me.

EXTREME CLOSE-UP *on pin with a soft shimmer of music.*

This friend of mine who kinda . . . disappeared . . . some years back.

Arthur's eyes flash up. The shimmer swells. Extreme CLOSE-UP *of Curt.*

>   (*very far-away*)
> I forget where we were. On a trip. But he says to me,
> 'Curt . . .

FLASH TO:

EXT. BEACH – DAY – 1973

A bleached-out image of Brian and Curt on some beach.

From a great distance, Brian is pinning something to Curt's shirt.

>   CURT
>   (*voice-over*)
> . . . A man's life is his image.'

CUT TO:

Brief, silent shots:

EXT. RAINBOW THEATRE – ROOF – MORNING – 1975

Urine streaming in a puddle.

CLOSE ON *Teenage Arthur watching Curt from behind. The remains of his Maxwell Demon make-up sully his face.*

Curt, standing peeing, turns.

BACK TO:

INT. MID-TOWN BAR – NEW YORK – NIGHT – 1984

The emerald pin, rolling loose in the palm of Curt's hand.

>   CURT
> Here. Why don't you hang on to it?

FLASH UP *to Arthur's face.*

ARTHUR

Me?

CURT

Why not? I've had it too long anyway. Go ahead.

Curt puts it in Arthur's hand. Arthur looks down at it, speechless.

(*tenderly*)

For your image.

Curt stands up, getting ready to go.

Arthur looks up at him, shaking his head.

Briefly: coins are pushed through slots, jukebox buttons pressed.

ARTHUR

Really. I couldn't. But thanks.

Arthur returns the pin with a polite smile.

Briefly: a jukebox forty-five drops into place.

Curt takes the pin, pockets it.

CURT

Whatever.

The introduction to '2HB'/Roxy Music begins on the jukebox.

RACK TO *Arthur*, CLOSE, *who turns toward the jukebox.*

The gay Latino Boy Teen recognizes the song.

LATINO BOY

Oh God, I love this song. Do you know this song?

GIRL

I don't think so.

Arthur turns back to Curt.

CURT

Anyway.

ARTHUR

Yeah.

                              CURT
        I'll see ya around.

                            ARTHUR
        Cheers.

Curt nods with a strange smile and turns.

Arthur watches him go. He reaches for his beer and finishes it off – and nearly gags. He spits something out in his hand.

CLOSE ON *the palm of his hand: the emerald pin lies covered in beer spittle.*

Arthur smiles, looking up in Curt's direction.

The front door is just swinging shut.

EXTREME CLOSE-UP *of Arthur.*

                            ARTHUR
                         (*voice-over*)
        He called it a freedom.

Briefly: Silent shots:

EXT. RAINBOW THEATRE – ROOF – MORNING – 1975

Curt, turning to camera while taking a piss (as before) Arthur, stretched out on the mattress, laughs.

        RETURN TO:

INT. MID-TOWN BAR – NEW YORK – NIGHT – 1984

Slow EXTREME CLOSE-UP *around Arthur's face, staring into the past.*

                            ARTHUR
                         (*voice-over*)
        A freedom you can allow yourself.

Arthur glances back into the main bar.

        Or not.

The first verse begins (sung by Jack Fairy), as Arthur closes the pin in his hand.

JACK
(*singing*)

Oh, I was moved by a screen demon . . .

DISSOLVE TO:

INT. RAINBOW THEATRE – NIGHT – 1975

Jack Fairy performs the glam-rock anthem with regal pathos, at the Death of Glitter Show.

Jack kneels at the edge of the stage under a single spot.

Arthur stands crushed in a corner, swaying to the music with Ray, Pearl and Billy.

Slow TRACK IN *on Mandy, watching from the wings.*

On-stage the lights shimmer gold as a mirror ball turns, conjuring a galaxy. Curt stands in the gleam with Polly Small, Malcolm from The Creatures, and Trevor, all singing along behind Jack.

We ascend, rising up from the stage, as a mist of glitter begins to fall. We pass the faces of glitter legends, projected onstage: Maxwell, Brian, Curt, Jack, Polly. We continue, rising into darkness.

DISSOLVE TO:

EXT. RAINBOW THEATRE – ROOF – DAWN – 1975

We pass through to the roof where it is dawn and snowing. Curt and Arthur are there, hanging out after sex. They turn in our direction but we continue our ascent.

DISSOLVE THROUGH:

A series of shots:

EXT. LONDON STREETS – DAY – 1974

Shots of busy Londoners on their way to work.

*[INT. ENGLISH FACTORY — DAY — 1974

Female Workers turn up a song on the radio, nodding their heads with the chorus.]

LONDON PUB — NIGHT — 1974

The song's chorus continues through a small transistor radio from which we TRACK, *revealing a candle-lit pub during the 1974 miners' strikes.*

TRACK *past the warm, flickering faces of Patrons, pints in hand, gazing solemnly toward the music.*

MONTAGE OF FACES (FROM BEFORE)

The three Young Punks, singing along to the chorus.

Two London Girls, arm in arm, singing.

The faces of New York Street Kids, looking up, some sadly, some angrily.

Boy with Crew Cut, eyes closed, sings a held note to the skies.

---

*Cut from completed film.

SLOW DISSOLVE TO:

*[EXT. LONDON DOCKS – AFTERNOON – 1974

The locked mouths of two handsome Dockers, kissing.

We begin a slow TRACK OUT *as the Dockers gently disengage. They look around, coolly, gradually drifting back to work. We begin ascending as well, as the song begins to fade. Gradually, the sweet strains of the music are replaced by the sounds of real life.*

In our ascent the small barge is revealed, surrounded by black, sparkling water. Finally the song has faded away (we hear ocean, birds) and the men have returned to their duties.]

HARD CUT TO BLACK:

'Make Me Smile'/Steve Harley Cockney Rebel over closing credits.

*Cut from completed film.

136

Storyboards

On the following pages is a
selection of storyboards which
were prepared for the shooting
of the film.

141